ONE DOUGH
A HUNDRED
COOKIES

ONE DOUGH
A HUNDRED
COOKIES

Linda Doeser

This edition published by Parragon Books Ltd in 2013
LOVE FOOD is an imprint of Parragon Books Ltd

Parragon Books Ltd
Chartist House
15–17 Trim Street
Bath BA1 1HA, UK
www.parragon.com/lovefood

Copyright © Parragon Books Ltd 2008 – 2013

ISBN 978-1-4723-3014-7

Printed in China

Written by Linda Doeser
Cover design by Geoff Borin
Internal design by Simon Levy
Photography by Clive Streeter
Home economy by Angela Drake, Teresa Goldfinch and Carole Streeter

Notes for the Reader
This book uses both metric and imperial measurements. Follow the same units of measurement throughout; do not mix metric and imperial. All spoon measurements are level: teaspoons are assumed to be 5 ml, and tablespoons are assumed to be 15 ml. Unless otherwise stated, milk is assumed to be full fat, eggs and individual vegetables are medium, and pepper is freshly ground black pepper.

Garnishes, decorations and serving suggestions are all optional and not necessarily included in the recipe ingredients or method. The times given are an approximate guide only. Preparation times differ according to the techniques used by different people and the cooking times may also vary from those given. Optional ingredients, variations or serving suggestions have not been included in the time calculations.

Recipes using raw or very lightly cooked eggs should be avoided by infants, the elderly, pregnant women, convalescents and anyone suffering from an illness. Pregnant and breastfeeding women are advised to avoid eating peanuts and peanut products. Sufferers from nut allergies should be aware that some of the ready-made ingredients used in the recipes in this book may contain nuts. Always check the packaging before use.

Contents

Basic Cookie Dough

Makes about 30

* 225 g/8 oz butter, softened
* 140 g/5 oz caster sugar
* 1 egg yolk, lightly beaten
* 2 tsp vanilla extract
* 280 g/10 oz plain flour
* salt

This is the recipe that all 100 variations of cookie in the book are based on.

For each recipe the basic mix is highlighted (*) for easy reference, so then all you have to do is follow the easy steps each time and a world of delicious and delectable cookies will await you.

Please note the basic ingredients may vary from time to time so please check these carefully.

Gooey

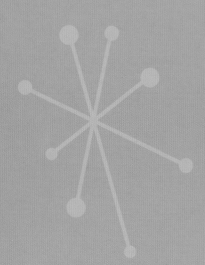

Double Choc Cookies

1. Preheat the oven to 190°C/375°F/Gas Mark 5. Line 2 baking sheets with baking parchment.

2. Put the butter and sugar into a bowl and mix well with a wooden spoon, then beat in the egg yolk and vanilla extract. Sift together the flour, cocoa and a pinch of salt into the mixture, add the chopped chocolate and sour cherries and stir until thoroughly combined.

3. Scoop up tablespoons of the mixture and shape into balls. Put them on the prepared baking sheets spaced well apart and flatten slightly.

4. Bake for 12–15 minutes. Leave to cool on the baking sheets for 5–10 minutes, then using a palette knife, carefully transfer to wire racks to cool completely.

Makes about 30

* 225 g/8 oz butter, softened
* 140 g/5 oz caster sugar
* 1 egg yolk, lightly beaten
* 2 tsp vanilla extract
* 250 g/9 oz plain flour
  25 g/1 oz cocoa powder
  350 g/12 oz dark chocolate, chopped
  55 g/2 oz dried sour cherries
* salt

Chocolate Fudge Squares

1. Put the butter and sugar into a bowl and mix well with a wooden spoon, then beat in the egg yolk and vanilla extract. Sift together the flour, cocoa and a pinch of salt into the mixture and stir until thoroughly combined. Halve the dough, shape into balls, wrap in clingfilm and chill in the refrigerator for 30–60 minutes.

2. Preheat the oven to 190°C/375°F/Gas Mark 5. Line 2 baking sheets with baking parchment.

3. Unwrap the dough and roll out between 2 sheets of baking parchment to about 3 mm/⅛ inch thick. Stamp out cookies with a 6-cm/2½-inch square cutter and put them on the prepared baking sheets spaced well apart.

4. Bake for 10–15 minutes, until golden brown. Leave to cool on the baking sheets for 5–10 minutes, then using a palette knife, carefully transfer the cookies to wire racks to cool completely.

5. For the chocolate fudge topping, put the fudge fingers into a heatproof bowl and melt over a pan of gently simmering water. Remove the bowl from the heat and gradually whisk in the cream. Leave to cool, then chill until spreadable. Spread the fudge topping over the cookies before serving.

Makes about 30

* 225 g/8 oz butter, softened
* 140 g/5 oz golden caster sugar
* 1 egg yolk, lightly beaten
* 2 tsp vanilla extract
* 225 g/8 oz plain flour
  55 g/2 oz cocoa powder
* salt

Chocolate fudge topping
8 chocolate-coated fudge fingers, broken into pieces
4 tbsp double cream

Mega Chip Cookies

1. Preheat the oven to 190°C/375°F/Gas Mark 5. Line 2–3 baking sheets with baking parchment.

2. Put the butter and sugar into a bowl and mix well with a wooden spoon, then beat in the egg yolk and vanilla extract. Sift together the flour, cocoa powder and a pinch of salt into the mixture, add both kinds of chocolate chips and stir until thoroughly combined.

3. Make 12 balls of the mixture, put them on to the prepared baking sheets, spaced well apart, and flatten slightly. Press the pieces of dark chocolate into the cookies.

4. Bake for 12–15 minutes. Leave to cool on the baking sheets for 5–10 minutes, then using a palette knife, carefully transfer to wire racks to cool completely.

Makes 12 large cookies

* 225 g/8 oz butter, softened
* 140 g/5 oz caster sugar
* 1 egg yolk, lightly beaten
* 2 tsp vanilla extract
* 225 g/8 oz plain flour
  55 g/2 oz cocoa powder
  85 g/3 oz milk chocolate chips
  85 g/3 oz white chocolate chips
  115 g/4 oz dark chocolate, coarsely chopped
* salt

Choco Mint Stars

1. Put the butter and sugar into a bowl and mix well with a wooden spoon, then beat in the egg yolk and peppermint extract. Sift together the flour and a pinch of salt into the mixture, add the coconut and stir until thoroughly combined. Divide the mixture in half, shape into balls and chill in the refrigerator for 30–60 minutes.

2. Preheat the oven to 190°C/375°F/Gas Mark 5. Line 2 baking sheets with baking parchment.

3. Unwrap the dough and roll out between 2 sheets of baking parchment to about 3 mm/⅛ inch thick and stamp out stars with a 6–7-cm/2½–2¾-inch cutter. Put them on the prepared baking sheets spaced well apart.

4. Bake for 10–12 minutes, until light golden brown. Leave to cool on the baking sheets for 5–10 minutes, then using a palette knife, carefully transfer the cookies to wire racks to cool completely.

5. Melt the white chocolate and the milk chocolate in separate heatproof bowls set over a pan of gently simmering water. Leave the cooled cookies on the racks and drizzle first with melted white chocolate and then with melted milk chocolate using a teaspoon. Leave to set.

Makes about 30

* 225 g/8 oz butter, softened
* 140 g/5 oz caster sugar
* 1 egg yolk, lightly beaten
  1 tsp peppermint extract
* 280 g/10 oz plain flour
  100 g/3½ oz desiccated coconut
  100 g/3½ oz white chocolate, broken into pieces
  100 g/3½ oz milk chocolate, broken into pieces
* salt

5

Almond & Raspberry Jam Drops

1. Preheat the oven to 190°C/375°F/Gas Mark 5. Line 2 baking sheets with baking parchment.

2. Put the butter and sugar into a bowl and mix well with a wooden spoon, then beat in the egg yolk and almond extract. Sift together the flour and a pinch of salt into the mixture, add the almonds and mixed peel and stir until thoroughly combined.

3. Scoop out tablespoons of the mixture and shape into balls with your hands, then put them on to the prepared baking sheets, spaced well apart. Use the dampened handle of a wooden spoon to make a hollow in the centre of each cookie and fill the hollows with raspberry jam.

4. Bake for 12–15 minutes, until golden brown. Leave to cool on the baking sheets for 5–10 minutes, then using a palette knife, carefully transfer the cookies to wire racks to cool completely.

Makes about 25

* 225 g/8 oz butter, softened
* 140 g/5 oz caster sugar
* 1 egg yolk, lightly beaten
  2 tsp almond extract
* 280 g/10 oz plain flour
  55 g/2 oz almonds, toasted and chopped
  55 g/2 oz chopped mixed peel
  4 tbsp raspberry jam
* salt

Orange & Chocolate Fingers

1. Put the butter, sugar and orange rind into a bowl and mix well with a wooden spoon, then beat in the egg yolk and orange juice. Sift together the flour, ginger and a pinch of salt into the mixture and stir until thoroughly combined. Shape the dough into a ball, wrap in clingfilm and chill in the refrigerator for 30–60 minutes.

2. Preheat the oven to 190°C/375°F/Gas Mark 5. Line 2 baking sheets with baking parchment.

3. Unwrap the dough and roll out between 2 sheets of baking parchment to a rectangle. Using a sharp knife, cut it into 10 x 2-cm/4 x ¾-inch strips and put them on the prepared baking sheets spaced well apart.

4. Bake for 10–12 minutes, until light golden brown. Leave to cool on the baking sheets for 5–10 minutes, then using a palette knife, carefully transfer to wire racks to cool completely.

5. Put the pieces of chocolate into a heatproof bowl and melt over a pan of gently simmering water, then remove from the heat and leave to cool. When the chocolate is cool but not set, dip the cookies diagonally into it to half coat, then put on the wire racks and leave to set. You may find it easier to do this using tongs.

Makes about 35

* 225 g/8 oz butter, softened
* 140 g/5 oz caster sugar
  grated rind of 1 orange
* 1 egg yolk, lightly beaten
  2 tsp orange juice
* 280 g/10 oz plain flour
  1 tsp ground ginger
  115 g/4 oz dark chocolate, broken into pieces
* salt

Traffic Lights

1. Put the butter and sugar into a bowl and mix well with a wooden spoon, then beat in the egg yolk and vanilla extract. Sift together the flour and a pinch of salt into the mixture, add the coconut and stir until thoroughly combined. Halve the dough, roll each piece into a ball, wrap in clingfilm and chill in the refrigerator for 30–60 minutes.

2. Preheat the oven to 190°C/375°F/Gas Mark 5. Line 2 baking sheets with baking parchment.

3. Roll out each piece of dough between 2 sheets of baking parchment to a rectangle about 5 mm/½ inch thick. Using a sharp knife, cut the dough into bars about 10 x 2-cm/ 4 x ¾-inch strips and put them on the prepared baking sheets spaced well apart.

4. Bake for 10–12 minutes, until golden brown. Leave to cool on the baking sheets for 5–10 minutes, then using a palette knife, carefully transfer the cookies to wire racks to cool completely.

5. To make the icing, mix together the egg white and lemon juice in a bowl, then gradually beat in the icing sugar until smooth. Leave the cooled cookies on the racks and spoon the icing over them. Decorate some with a vertical row of red, yellow and green glacé cherries for traffic lights. For pedestrian lights, put a red jelly baby at the top of a cookie and a green one at the bottom. Leave to set.

Makes about 35–40

* 225 g/8 oz butter, softened
* 140 g/5 oz caster sugar
* 1 egg yolk, lightly beaten
* 2 tsp vanilla extract
* 280 g/10 oz plain flour, plus extra for dusting
  100 g/3½ oz desiccated coconut
* salt

To decorate
1½ tbsp lightly beaten egg white
1½ tbsp lemon juice
175 g/6 oz icing sugar
red, yellow and green glacé cherries
red and green jelly babies

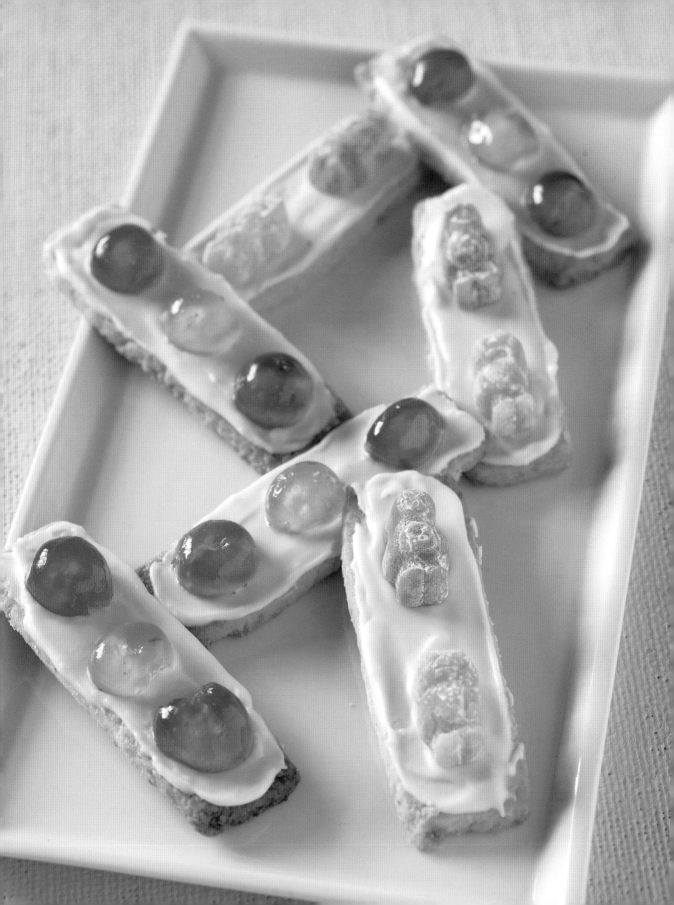

Sticky Ginger Cookies

1. Put the butter and sugar into a bowl and mix well with a wooden spoon, then beat in the egg yolk and ginger syrup. Sift together the flour and a pinch of salt into the mixture, add the stem ginger and chocolate chips and stir until thoroughly combined. Shape the mixture into a log, wrap in clingfilm and chill in the refrigerator for 30–60 minutes.

2. Preheat the oven to 190°C/375°F/Gas Mark 5. Line 2 baking sheets with baking parchment.

3. Unwrap the log and cut it into 5-mm/¼-inch slices with a sharp serrated knife. Put them on to the prepared baking sheets spaced well apart.

4. Bake for 12–15 minutes, until golden brown. Leave to cool on the baking sheets for 5–10 minutes, then using a palette knife, carefully transfer the cookies to wire racks to cool completely.

Makes 20

* 225 g/8 oz butter, softened
* 140 g/5 oz golden caster sugar
* 1 egg yolk, lightly beaten
  55 g/2 oz stem ginger, coarsely chopped, plus 1 tbsp syrup from the jar
* 280 g/10 oz plain flour
  55 g/2 oz plain chocolate chips
* salt

Peanut Butter & Grape Jelly Cookies

1. Preheat the oven to 190°C/375°F/Gas Mark 5. Line 2 baking sheets with baking parchment.

2. Put the butter and sugar into a bowl and mix well with a wooden spoon, then beat in the egg yolk, vanilla extract and peanut butter. Sift together the flour and a pinch of salt into the mixture and stir until thoroughly combined.

3. Scoop out tablespoons of the mixture and shape into balls with your hands, then put them on to the prepared baking sheets spaced well apart. Use the dampened handle of a wooden spoon to make a hollow in the centre of each cookie and fill the hollows with grape jelly.

4. Bake for 12–15 minutes, until golden brown. Leave to cool on the baking sheets for 5–10 minutes, then using a palette knife, carefully transfer the cookies to wire racks to cool completely.

Makes about 25

* 225 g/8 oz butter, softened
* 140 g/5 oz caster sugar
* 1 egg yolk, lightly beaten
* 2 tsp vanilla extract
  100 g/3½ oz crunchy peanut butter
* 280 g/10 oz plain flour
  4 tbsp grape jelly
* salt

Caramel Glaze Cookies

1. Put the butter and sugar into a bowl and mix well with a wooden spoon, then beat in the egg yolk and vanilla extract. Sift together the flour and a pinch of salt into the mixture and stir until thoroughly combined. Halve the dough, shape into balls, wrap in clingfilm and chill in the refrigerator for 30–60 minutes.

2. For the caramel glaze, put the sugar and lemon juice into a saucepan and add 1½ tablespoons water. Heat gently, stirring constantly, until the sugar has dissolved, then boil, without stirring, until a rich caramel colour. Remove the pan from the heat and plunge the base into a bowl of cold water. Stir in a further 3 tablespoons of cold water and set the caramel aside to cool completely.

3. Line 2 baking sheets with baking parchment. Unwrap the dough and roll out to about 3 mm/⅛ inch thick. Stamp out rounds with a 6-cm/2½-inch fluted cutter and put them on the prepared baking sheets.

4. Preheat the oven to 190°C/375°F/Gas Mark 5.

5. Beat the egg yolk with 1 tbsp of the caramel in a bowl and brush the glaze over the cookies. Leave to dry, then brush with the glaze again. Repeat, then brush the cookies with the glaze for a fourth time and make a pattern with a fork. Bake the cookies for 10–12 minutes, until golden brown. Leave to cool for 5–10 minutes, then carefully transfer to wire racks to cool completely.

Makes about 30

* 225 g/8 oz butter, softened
* 140 g/5 oz caster sugar
* 1 egg yolk, lightly beaten
* 2 tsp vanilla extract
* 280 g/10 oz plain flour
* salt

Caramel glaze
55 g/2 oz sugar
½ tsp lemon juice
1 egg yolk

Pear & Mint Cookies

1. Put the butter and sugar into a bowl and mix well with a wooden spoon, then beat in the egg yolk and vanilla extract. Sift together the flour and a pinch of salt into the mixture, add the pears and stir until thoroughly combined. Shape the mixture into a log, wrap in clingfilm and chill in the refrigerator for 30–60 minutes.

2. Preheat the oven to 190°C/375°F/Gas Mark 5. Line 2 baking sheets with baking parchment.

3. Unwrap the log and cut it into 5-mm/¼-inch slices with a sharp serrated knife. Put them on to the prepared baking sheets spaced well apart.

4. Bake for 10–15 minutes, until golden brown. Leave to cool on the baking sheets for 5–10 minutes, then using a palette knife, carefully transfer the cookies to wire racks to cool completely.

5. To decorate, sift the icing sugar into a bowl and stir in the peppermint extract. Gradually stir in the hot water until the icing has the consistency of double cream. Leave the cooled cookies on the wire racks and drizzle lines of icing over them, using a teaspoon. Leave to set.

Makes about 30

- 225 g/8 oz butter, softened
- 140 g/5 oz caster sugar
- 1 egg yolk, lightly beaten
- 2 tsp vanilla extract
- 280 g/10 oz plain flour
- 100 g/3½ oz dried pears, finely chopped
- salt

To decorate
- 115 g/4 oz icing sugar
- few drops of peppermint extract
- 1 tbsp hot water

Chocolate, Date & Pecan Nut Pinwheels

1. Put the butter and 140 g/5 oz of the sugar into a bowl and mix well with a wooden spoon, then beat in the egg yolk. Sift together the flour, cocoa powder and a pinch of salt into the mixture, add the pecan nuts and stir until thoroughly combined. Halve the dough, shape into balls, wrap in clingfilm and chill for 30–60 minutes.

2. Meanwhile, put the dried dates, orange rind, orange flower water and remaining sugar into a saucepan and cook over a low heat, stirring constantly, until the sugar has dissolved. Bring to the boil, then lower the heat and simmer, stirring occasionally, for 5 minutes. Remove the pan from the heat, pour the mixture into a bowl and leave to cool, then chill in the refrigerator.

3. Unwrap the dough and roll out between 2 pieces of baking parchment to rectangles about 5 mm/¼ inch thick. Spread the date filling evenly over the rectangles. Roll up the dough from a short side like a Swiss roll, wrap in the baking parchment and chill for a further 30 minutes.

4. Preheat the oven to 190°C/375°F/Gas Mark 5. Line 2 baking sheets with baking parchment.

5. Unwrap the rolls and cut into 1-cm/½-in slices. Put them on the prepared baking sheets and bake for 15–20 minutes, until golden brown. Leave to cool on the baking sheets for 5–10 minutes, then carefully transfer to wire racks to cool completely.

Makes about 30

- 225 g/8 oz butter, softened
- 200 g/7 oz caster sugar
- 1 egg yolk, lightly beaten
- 225 g/8 oz plain flour
- 55 g/2 oz cocoa powder
- 100 g/3½ oz pecan nuts, finely ground
- 280 g/10 oz dried dates, coarsely chopped
- finely grated rind of 1 orange
- 175 ml/6 fl oz orange flower water
- salt

Cinnamon & Caramel Cookies

1. Preheat the oven to 190°C/375°F/Gas Mark 5. Line 2 baking sheets with baking parchment.

2. Put the butter and sugar into a bowl and mix well with a wooden spoon, then beat in the egg yolk and vanilla extract. Sift together the flour, cinnamon, allspice and a pinch of salt into the mixture and stir until thoroughly combined.

3. Scoop up tablespoons of the mixture, shape into balls and place on the prepared baking sheets spaced well apart. Bake for 8 minutes. Place a caramel sweet on top of each cookie, return to the oven and bake for a further 6–7 minutes.

4. Remove from the oven and leave to cool on the baking sheets for 5–10 minutes. Using a palette knife, carefully transfer the cookies to wire racks to cool completely.

Makes about 25

- 225 g/8 oz butter, softened
- 140 g/5 oz caster sugar
- 1 egg yolk, lightly beaten
- 1 tsp vanilla extract
- 280 g/10 oz plain flour
- 1 tsp ground cinnamon
- ½ tsp allspice
- 25–30 caramel sweets
- salt

Marshmallow Daisies

1. Put the butter and sugar into a bowl and mix well with a wooden spoon, then beat in the egg yolk and vanilla extract. Sift together the flour, cocoa powder and a pinch of salt into the mixture and stir until thoroughly combined. Halve the dough, roll each piece into a ball, wrap in clingfilm and chill in the refrigerator for 30–60 minutes.

2. Preheat the oven to 190°C/375°F/Gas Mark 5. Line 2 baking sheets with baking parchment.

3. Unwrap the dough and roll out between 2 sheets of baking parchment to about 1 cm/½ inch thick and stamp out about 30 cookies with a 5-cm/2-in flower cutter. Put them on the prepared baking sheets spaced well apart.

4. Bake for 10–12 minutes, until firm. Remove the baking sheets from the oven but do not turn off the heat. Arrange the pieces of marshmallow over the petals of the flowers, cutting them to fit if necessary. Return to the oven for 30–60 seconds, until the marshmallow has softened.

5. Leave to cool on the baking sheets for 5–10 minutes, then using a palette knife, carefully transfer the cookies to wire racks to cool completely. Meanwhile, heat the jam in a small saucepan, strain into a bowl and leave to cool. Pipe a small circle of jam in the centre of each flower and top with the sugar sprinkles.

Makes about 30

* 225 g/8 oz butter, softened
* 140 g/5 oz caster sugar
* 1 egg yolk, lightly beaten
* 2 tsp vanilla extract
* 225 g/8 oz plain flour
  55 g/2 oz cocoa powder
  about 90 white mini marshmallows, halved horizontally
  4 tbsp peach jam
  4 tbsp yellow sugar sprinkles
* salt

Peanut Partners

1. Put the butter and sugar into a bowl and mix well with a wooden spoon, then beat in the egg yolk. Sift together the flour, ginger and a pinch of salt into the mixture, add the lemon rind and stir until thoroughly combined. Halve the dough, shape into balls, wrap in clingfilm and chill in the refrigerator for 30–60 minutes.

2. Preheat the oven to 190°C/375°F/Gas Mark 5. Line 2 baking sheets with baking parchment.

3. Unwrap the dough and roll out between 2 sheets of baking parchment to about 3 mm/⅛ inch thick. Stamp out rounds with a 6-cm/2½-inch fluted cutter and put them on the prepared baking sheets spaced well apart.

4. Bake for 10–15 minutes, until golden brown. Leave to cool on the baking sheets for 5–10 minutes, then using a palette knife, carefully transfer the cookies to wire racks to cool completely.

5. Beat together the peanut butter and icing sugar in a bowl, adding a little water if necessary. Spread the cookies with the peanut butter mixture and decorate with whole or chopped peanuts.

Makes about 30

* 225 g/8 oz butter, softened
* 140 g/5 oz caster sugar
* 1 egg yolk, lightly beaten
* 280 g/10 oz plain flour
  1 tsp ground ginger
  2 tsp finely grated lemon rind
  3 tbsp smooth peanut butter
  3 tbsp icing sugar
* salt
  whole or chopped roasted peanuts, to decorate

Melt-in-the middles

1. Preheat the oven to 190°C/375°F/Gas Mark 5. Line 2 baking sheets with baking parchment.

2. For the middle filling, whisk the egg white until soft peaks form, then gradually whisk in the sugar. Gently fold in the coconut, flour and papaya. Set aside.

3. Melt the chocolate in a heatproof bowl set over a pan of barely simmering water, then remove from the heat. Put the butter and sugar into a bowl and mix well, then beat in the egg yolk and vanilla extract. Sift together the flour, cocoa powder and a pinch of salt into the mixture and stir until thoroughly combined. Stir in the melted chocolate and knead lightly.

4. Roll out the dough between 2 sheets of baking parchment to 5–8 mm/¼–⅜ inch thick. Stamp out rounds with a 7-cm/2¾-inch fluted round cutter and put them on the prepared baking sheets. Using a 3-cm/1¼-inch plain round cutter, stamp out the centres and remove them. Bake for 8 minutes, then remove the baking sheets from the oven and lower the temperature to 160°C/325°F/Gas Mark 3. Spoon the middle mixture into the centre of the cookies. Crumple 2 sheets of foil and place them over the baking sheets but without their touching the cookies.

5. Return to the oven and bake for a further 15–20 minutes, until the middles are firm. Leave to cool on the baking sheets for 5–10 minutes, then carefully transfer to wire racks to cool completely.

Makes about 30

85 g/3 oz dark chocolate, broken into pieces
* 115 g/4 oz butter, softened
* 140 g/5 oz golden caster sugar
* 1 egg yolk, lightly beaten
* 2 tsp vanilla extract
* 280 g/10 oz plain flour
1 tbsp cocoa powder
* salt

Middle filling
1 egg white
55 g/2 oz caster sugar
85 g/3 oz desiccated coconut
1 tsp plain flour
2 tbsp finely chopped ready-to-eat dried papaya

Chocolate Sprinkle Cookies

1. Put the butter and sugar into a bowl and mix well with a wooden spoon, then beat in the egg yolk and vanilla extract. Sift together the flour, cocoa powder and a pinch of salt into the mixture and stir until thoroughly combined. Halve the dough, roll each piece into a ball, wrap in clingfilm and chill in the refrigerator for 30–60 minutes to firm up.

2. Preheat the oven to 190°C/375°F/Gas Mark 5. Line 2 baking sheets with baking parchment.

3. Unwrap the dough and roll out between 2 pieces of baking parchment to about 5 mm/¼ inch thick and stamp out 30 cookies with a 6–7-cm/2½–2¾-inch fluted round cutter. Put them on the prepared baking sheets spaced well apart.

4. Bake for 10–12 minutes. Leave to cool on the baking sheets for 5–10 minutes, then using a palette knife, carefully transfer the cookies to wire racks to cool completely.

5. Put the pieces of white chocolate into a heatproof bowl and melt over a pan of gently simmering water, then immediately remove from the heat. Spread the melted chocolate over the cookies, leave to cool slightly and then sprinkle with the chocolate vermicelli. Leave to cool and set.

Makes about 30

* 225 g/8 oz butter, softened
* 140 g/5 oz caster sugar
* 1 egg yolk, lightly beaten
* 2 tsp vanilla extract
* 225 g/8 oz plain flour, plus extra for dusting
  55 g/2 oz cocoa powder
  200 g/7 oz white chocolate, broken into pieces
  85 g/3 oz chocolate vermicelli
* salt

Treacle & Spice Drizzles

1. Put the butter, treacle and sugar into a bowl and mix well with a wooden spoon, then beat in the egg yolk. Sift together the flour, cinnamon, nutmeg, cloves and a pinch of salt into the mixture, add the walnuts and stir until thoroughly combined. Halve the dough, shape into balls, wrap in clingfilm and chill in the refrigerator for 30–60 minutes.

2. Preheat the oven to 190°C/375°F/Gas Mark 5. Line 2 baking sheets with baking parchment.

3. Unwrap the dough and roll out between 2 sheets of baking parchment to about 5 mm/¼ inch thick. Stamp out rounds with a 6-cm/2½-inch fluted cutter and put them on the prepared baking sheets.

4. Bake for 10–15 minutes, until firm. Leave to cool on the baking sheets for 5–10 minutes, then using a palette knife, carefully transfer the cookies to wire racks to cool completely.

5. For the icing, sift the icing sugar into a bowl, then gradually stir in the hot water until the icing has the consistency of thick cream. Spoon half the icing into another bowl and stir a few drops of yellow food colouring into one bowl and a few drops of pink food colouring into the other. Leave the cookies on the racks and, using teaspoons, drizzle the yellow icing over them in one direction and the pink icing over them at right angles. Leave to set.

Makes about 25

* 200 g/7 oz butter, softened
  2 tbsp black treacle
* 140 g/5 oz caster sugar
* 1 egg yolk, lightly beaten
* 280 g/10 oz plain flour
  1 tsp ground cinnamon
  ½ tsp grated nutmeg
  ½ tsp ground cloves
  2 tbsp chopped walnuts
* salt

Icing
115 g/4 oz icing sugar
1 tbsp hot water
a few drops of yellow food colouring
a few drops of pink food colouring

Chewy Candied Fruit Cookies

1. Put the butter and sugar into a bowl and mix well with a wooden spoon, then beat in the egg yolk and vanilla extract. Sift together the flour and a pinch of salt into the mixture and stir until thoroughly combined. Halve the dough, shape into balls, wrap in clingfilm and chill for 30–60 minutes.

2. Preheat the oven to 190°C/375°F/Gas Mark 5. Line 2 baking sheets with baking parchment.

3. Unwrap the dough and roll out between 2 sheets of baking parchment. Stamp out rounds with a 6-cm/2½-inch plain round cutter and put them on the prepared baking sheets spaced well apart.

4. For the candied topping, put the syrup, butter and sugar into a saucepan and melt over a low heat, stirring occasionally. Meanwhile, put the fruit, mixed peel, nuts and flour into a bowl and mix well. When the syrup mixture is thoroughly combined, stir it into the fruit mixture. Divide the candied topping among the cookies, gently spreading it out to the edges.

5. Bake for 10–15 minutes, until firm. Leave to cool on the baking sheets for 5–10 minutes, then using a palette knife, carefully transfer the cookies to wire racks to cool completely.

Makes about 30

* 225 g/8 oz butter, softened
* 140 g/5 oz caster sugar
* 1 egg yolk, lightly beaten
* 2 tsp vanilla extract
* 280 g/10 oz plain flour
* salt

Candied topping
4 tbsp maple syrup
55 g/2 oz butter
55 g/2 oz caster sugar
115 g/4 oz ready-to-eat dried peaches, chopped
55 g/2 oz glacé cherries, chopped
55 g/2 oz chopped mixed peel
85 g/3 oz macadamia nuts, chopped
25 g/1 oz plain flour

Chocolate Spread & Hazelnut Drops

1. Preheat the oven to 190°C/375°F/Gas Mark 5. Line 2 baking sheets with baking parchment.

2. Put the butter and sugar into a bowl and mix well with a wooden spoon, then beat in the egg yolk and vanilla extract. Sift together the flour, cocoa and a pinch of salt into the mixture, add the ground hazelnuts and stir until thoroughly combined.

3. Scoop out tablespoons of the mixture and shape into balls with your hands, then put them on to the prepared baking sheets spaced well apart. Use the dampened handle of a wooden spoon to make a hollow in the centre of each cookie.

4. Bake for 12–15 minutes. Leave to cool on the baking sheets for 5–10 minutes, then using a palette knife, carefully transfer the cookies to wire racks to cool completely. When they are cold fill the hollows in the centre with chocolate and hazelnut spread.

Makes about 30

* 225 g/8 oz butter, softened
* 140 g/5 oz caster sugar
* 1 egg yolk, lightly beaten
* 2 tsp vanilla extract
* 225 g/8 oz plain flour
  55 g/2 oz cocoa powder
  55 g/2 oz ground hazelnuts
  55 g/2 oz plain chocolate chips
  4 tbsp chocolate and hazelnut spread
* salt

Crunch

Chocolate Chip & Cinnamon Cookies

1. Preheat the oven to 190°C/375°F/Gas Mark 5. Line 2 baking sheets with baking parchment.

2. Put the butter and sugar into a bowl and mix well with a wooden spoon, then beat in the egg yolk and orange extract. Sift together the flour and a pinch of salt into the mixture, add the chocolate chips and stir until thoroughly combined.

3. For the cinnamon coating, mix together the caster sugar and cinnamon in a shallow dish. Scoop out tablespoons of the cookie dough, roll them into balls, then roll them in the cinnamon mixture to coat. Put them on the prepared baking sheets spaced well apart.

4. Bake for 12–15 minutes. Leave to cool on the baking sheets for 5–10 minutes, then using a palette knife, carefully transfer to wire racks to cool completely.

Makes about 30

- 225 g/8 oz butter, softened
- 140 g/5 oz caster sugar
- 1 egg yolk, lightly beaten
- 2 tsp orange extract
- 280 g/10 oz plain flour
- 100 g/3½ oz plain chocolate chips
- salt

Cinnamon coating
1½ tbsp caster sugar
1½ tbsp ground cinnamon

Almond Crunchies

1. Put the butter and sugar into a bowl and mix well with a wooden spoon, then beat in the egg yolk and almond extract. Sift together the flour and a pinch of salt into the mixture, add the almonds and stir until thoroughly combined. Halve the dough, shape it into balls, wrap in clingfilm and chill in the refrigerator for 30–60 minutes.

2. Preheat the oven to 190°C/375°F/Gas Mark 5. Line 2–3 baking sheets with baking parchment.

3. Shape the dough into about 50 small balls and flatten them slightly between the palms of your hands. Put on the prepared baking sheets spaced well apart.

4. Bake for 15–20 minutes, until golden brown. Leave to cool on the baking sheets for 5–10 minutes, then using a palette knife, carefully transfer to wire racks to cool completely.

Makes about 50

* 225 g/8 oz butter, softened
* 140 g/5 oz caster sugar
* 1 egg yolk, lightly beaten
  ½ tsp almond extract
* 225 g/8 oz plain flour
  225 g/8 oz blanched almonds, chopped
* salt

Flower Gems

1. Put the butter and sugar into a bowl and mix well with a wooden spoon, then beat in the egg yolk and lemon juice. Sift together the flour and a pinch of salt into the mixture, add the tea leaves and stir until thoroughly combined. Halve the dough, shape it into balls, wrap in clingfilm and chill in the refrigerator for 30–60 minutes.

2. Preheat the oven to 190°C/375°F/Gas Mark 5. Line 2 baking sheets with baking parchment.

3. Roll out the dough between 2 sheets of baking parchment to about 3 mm/⅛ inch thick. Stamp out flowers with a 5-cm/ 2-inch flower cutter. Put them on the prepared baking sheets spaced well apart.

4. Bake for 10–12 minutes, until golden brown. Leave to cool on the baking sheets for 5–10 minutes, then carefully transfer the cookies to wire racks to cool completely.

5. To decorate, mix the lemon juice with 1 tbsp water in a bowl, then gradually stir in enough icing sugar to make a mixture with the consistency of thick cream. Divide the icing among 4 separate bowls and add a drop of different food colouring to each.

6. Leave the cookies on the racks. Spread orange icing on a quarter of the cookies, pink on another quarter and so on. When the icing is beginning to set, add a matching flower in the centre of each. Leave to cool.

Makes about 30

* 225 g/8 oz butter, softened
* 140 g/5 oz caster sugar
* 1 egg yolk, lightly beaten
  1 tsp lemon juice
* 280 g/10 oz plain flour
  2 tbsp jasmine tea leaves
* salt

To decorate
1 tbsp lemon juice
200 g/7 oz icing sugar
orange, pink, blue and yellow food colouring
orange, pink, blue and yellow sugar flowers

24

Snickerdoodles

1. Put the butter and sugar into a bowl and mix well with a wooden spoon, then beat in the eggs and vanilla extract. Sift together the flour, bicarbonate of soda, nutmeg and a pinch of salt into the mixture, add the pecan nuts and stir until thoroughly combined. Shape the dough into a ball, wrap in clingfilm and chill in the refrigerator for 30–60 minutes.

2. Preheat the oven to 190°C/375°F/Gas Mark 5. Line 2–3 baking sheets with baking parchment.

3. For the cinnamon coating, mix together the caster sugar and cinnamon in a shallow dish. Scoop up tablespoons of the cookie dough and roll into balls. Roll each ball in the cinnamon mixture to coat and place on the prepared baking sheets spaced well apart.

4. Bake for 10–12 minutes, until golden brown. Leave to cool on the baking sheets for 5–10 minutes, then using a palette knife, carefully transfer to wire racks to cool completely.

Makes about 40

* 225 g/8 oz butter, softened
* 140 g/5 oz caster sugar
* 2 large eggs, lightly beaten
* 1 tsp vanilla extract
* 400 g/14 oz plain flour
  1 tsp bicarbonate of soda
  ½ tsp freshly grated nutmeg
  55 g/2 oz pecan nuts, finely chopped
* salt

Cinnamon coating
1 tbsp caster sugar
2 tbsp ground cinnamon

25

Lavender Cookies

1. Preheat the oven to 190°C/375°F/Gas Mark 5. Line 2 baking sheets with baking parchment.

2. Put the butter and sugar into a bowl and mix well with a wooden spoon, then beat in the egg. Sift together the flour and baking powder into the mixture, add the lavender and stir until thoroughly combined.

3. Put tablespoons of the mixture on to the prepared baking sheets spaced well apart. Bake for 15 minutes, until golden brown. Leave to cool on the baking sheets for 5–10 minutes, then using a palette knife, carefully transfer to wire racks to cool completely.

Makes about 40

* 225 g/8 oz butter, softened
* 175 g/6 oz caster sugar
* 1 large egg, lightly beaten
* 250 g/9 oz plain flour
  2 tsp baking powder
  1 tbsp dried lavender, chopped

Rose Flower Cookies

1. Put the butter and sugar into a bowl and mix well with a wooden spoon, then beat in the egg and rose water. Sift together the flour, baking powder and a pinch of salt into the mixture and stir until thoroughly combined. Shape the dough into a log, wrap in clingfilm and chill in the refrigerator for 1–2 hours.

2. Preheat the oven to 190°C/375°F/Gas Mark 5. Line 2–3 baking sheets with baking parchment.

3. Unwrap the dough and cut into thin slices with a sharp serrated knife. Put on the prepared baking sheets spaced well apart. Bake for 10–12 minutes, until light golden brown. Leave the cookies to cool on the baking sheets for 10 minutes, then using a palette knife, carefully transfer them to wire racks to cool completely.

4. To make the icing, lightly beat the egg white with a fork in a bowl. Sift in half the icing sugar and stir well, then sift in the remaining icing sugar and flour and mix in sufficient rose water to make a smooth, easy-to-spread icing. Stir in a few drops of pink food colouring.

5. Leave the cookies on the racks. Gently spread the icing over them and leave to set.

Makes about 55–60

* 225 g/8 oz butter, softened
* 225 g/8 oz caster sugar
* 1 large egg, lightly beaten
* 1 tbsp rose water
* 280 g/10 oz plain flour
* 1 tsp baking powder
* salt

Icing
1 egg white
250 g/9 oz icing sugar
2 tsp plain flour
2 tsp rose water
pink food colouring

Alphabet Cookies

1. Put the butter and sugar into a bowl and mix well with a wooden spoon, then beat in the egg yolk and grenadine. Sift together the flour and a pinch of salt into the mixture and stir until thoroughly combined. Halve the dough, shape into balls, wrap in clingfilm and chill in the refrigerator for 30–60 minutes.

2. Preheat the oven to 190°C/375°F/Gas Mark 5. Line 2 baking sheets with baking parchment.

3. Unwrap the dough and roll out between 2 sheets of baking parchment to about 3 mm/⅛ inch thick. Sprinkle half the seeds over each piece of dough and lightly roll the rolling pin over them. Stamp out letters with alphabet cutters and put them on the prepared baking sheets spaced well apart.

4. Bake for 10–12 minutes, until golden brown. Leave to cool on the baking sheets for 5–10 minutes, then using a palette knife, carefully transfer the cookies to wire racks to cool completely.

Makes about 30

- ✳ 225 g/8 oz butter, softened
- ✳ 140 g/5 oz caster sugar
- ✳ 1 egg yolk, lightly beaten
  2 tsp grenadine
- ✳ 280 g/10 oz plain flour
  5–6 tbsp unsalted dried pomegranate seeds or roasted melon seeds
- ✳ salt

28

Number Crunchers

1. Put the butter and sugar into a bowl and mix well with a wooden spoon, then beat in the egg yolk and vanilla extract. Sift together the flour, ginger, cinnamon, cloves and a pinch of salt into the mixture and stir until thoroughly combined. Halve the dough, shape into balls, wrap in clingfilm and chill in the refrigerator for 30–60 minutes.

2. Preheat the oven to 190°C/375°F/Gas Mark 5. Line 2 baking sheets with baking parchment.

3. Unwrap the dough and roll out between 2 sheets of baking parchment to about 3 mm/⅛ inch thick. Sprinkle half the nuts over each piece of dough and lightly roll the rolling pin over them. Stamp out numbers with number shape cutters and put them on the prepared baking sheets spaced well apart.

4. Bake for 10–12 minutes, until golden brown. Leave to cool on the baking sheets for 5–10 minutes, then using a palette knife, carefully transfer the cookies to wire racks to cool completely.

Makes about 35

* 225 g/8 oz butter, softened
* 140 g/5 oz caster sugar
* 1 egg yolk, lightly beaten
* 2 tsp vanilla extract
* 280 g/10 oz plain flour
  1 tsp ground ginger
  ¼ tsp ground cinnamon
  ¼ tsp ground cloves
  4–5 tbsp chopped macadamia nuts
* salt

Fennel & Angelica Cookies

1. Put the butter and sugar into a bowl and mix well with a wooden spoon, then beat in the egg yolk and angelica. Sift together the flour and a pinch of salt into the mixture, add the fennel seeds and stir until thoroughly combined. Shape the dough into a log, wrap in clingfilm and chill in the refrigerator for 30–60 minutes.

2. Preheat the oven to 190°C/375°F/Gas Mark 5. Line 2 baking sheets with baking parchment.

3. Unwrap the dough and cut into 1-cm/½-inch slices with a sharp serrated knife. Put them on the prepared baking sheets spaced well apart.

4. Bake for 12–15 minutes, until golden brown. Leave to cool on the baking sheets for 5–10 minutes, then using a palette knife, carefully transfer to wire racks to cool completely.

Makes about 20

* 225 g/8 oz butter, softened
* 140 g/5 oz caster sugar
* 1 egg yolk, lightly beaten
  1 tbsp finely chopped angelica
* 280 g/10 oz plain flour
  1 tbsp fennel seeds
* salt

Cashew & Poppy Seed Cookies

1. Put the butter and sugar into a bowl and mix well with a wooden spoon, then beat in the egg yolk. Sift together the flour, cinnamon and a pinch of salt into the mixture, add the nuts and stir until thoroughly combined. Shape the dough into a log. Spread out the poppy seeds in a shallow dish and roll the log in them until well coated. Wrap in clingfilm and chill in the refrigerator for 30–60 minutes.

2. Preheat the oven to 190°C/375°F/Gas Mark 5. Line 2 baking sheets with baking parchment.

3. Unwrap the dough and cut into 1-cm/½-inch slices with a sharp serrated knife. Put them on the prepared baking sheets and bake for 12 minutes, until golden brown. Leave to cool on the baking sheets for 5–10 minutes, then using a palette knife, carefully transfer to wire racks to cool completely.

Makes about 20

* 225 g/8 oz butter, softened
* 140 g/5 oz caster sugar
* 1 egg yolk, lightly beaten
* 280 g/10 oz plain flour
  1 tsp ground cinnamon
  115 g/4 oz cashew nuts, chopped
  2–3 tbsp poppy seeds
* salt

31

Lemon & Sesame Seed Cookies

1. Dry-fry the sesame seeds in a heavy-based frying pan over a low heat, stirring frequently, for 2–3 minutes, until they give off their aroma. Remove the pan from the heat and set aside to cool.

2. Put the butter, sugar, lemon rind and toasted seeds into a bowl and mix well with a wooden spoon, then beat in the egg yolk. Sift together the flour and a pinch of salt into the mixture and stir until thoroughly combined. Halve the dough, form it into balls, wrap in clingfilm and chill in the refrigerator for 30–60 minutes.

3. Preheat the oven to 190°C/375°F/Gas Mark 5. Line 2 baking sheets with baking parchment.

4. Unwrap the dough and roll out between 2 sheets of baking parchment. Stamp out rounds with a 6-cm/2½-inch cutter and put them on the prepared baking sheets spaced well apart. Bake for 10–12 minutes, until light golden brown. Leave to cool on the baking sheets for 5–10 minutes, then using a palette knife, carefully transfer the cookies to wire racks to cool completely.

5. For the icing, sift the icing sugar into a bowl, add the lemon extract and gradually stir in the hot water until the icing is smooth and has the consistency of thick cream. Leave the cooled cookies on the racks and spread the icing over them. Leave to set.

Makes about 30

2 tbsp sesame seeds
225 g/8 oz butter, softened
140 g/5 oz caster sugar
1 tbsp finely grated lemon rind
1 egg yolk, lightly beaten
280 g/10 oz plain flour
salt

Icing
115 g/4 oz icing sugar
few drops of lemon extract
1 tbsp hot water

Walnut & Coffee Cookies

1. Put the instant latte into a bowl and stir in the hot water to make a paste. Put the butter and sugar into a bowl and mix well with a wooden spoon, then beat in the egg yolk and coffee paste. Sift together the flour and a pinch of salt into the mixture, add the walnuts and stir until thoroughly combined. Halve the dough, shape into balls, wrap in clingfilm and chill in the refrigerator for 30–60 minutes.

2. Preheat the oven to 190°C/375°F/Gas Mark 5. Line 2 baking sheets with baking parchment.

3. Unwrap the dough and roll out between 2 sheets of baking parchment to about 3 mm/⅛ inch thick. Stamp out rounds with a 6-cm/2½-inch cutter and put them on the prepared baking sheets spaced well apart.

4. Lightly brush the cookies with water, sprinkle with the coffee sugar crystals and bake for 10–12 minutes. Leave to cool on the baking sheets for 5–10 minutes, then using a palette knife, carefully transfer the cookies to wire racks to cool completely.

Makes about 30

2 sachets instant latte

1 tbsp hot water

✳ 225 g/8 oz butter, softened

✳ 140 g/5 oz caster sugar

✳ 1 egg yolk, lightly beaten

✳ 280 g/10 oz plain flour

100 g/3½ oz walnuts, finely chopped

✳ salt

coffee sugar crystals, for sprinkling

Neapolitan Cookies

1. Put the butter and sugar into a bowl and mix well with a wooden spoon, then beat in the egg yolk. Divide the mixture equally among 3 bowls.

2. Beat the vanilla extract into the first bowl. Sift together one-third of the flour and a pinch of salt into the mixture and stir until combined. Shape into a ball, wrap in clingfilm and chill in the refrigerator for 30–60 minutes. Sift together one-third of the flour, the cocoa powder and a pinch of salt into the second bowl and stir until combined. Shape into a ball, wrap in clingfilm and chill in the refrigerator.

3. Beat the almond extract into the third bowl. Sift together the flour and a pinch of salt and stir until combined. Mix in a few drops of green food colouring, then form into a ball, wrap in clingfilm and chill in the refrigerator. Preheat the oven to 190°C/375°F/ Gas Mark 5. Line 2 baking sheets with baking parchment.

4. Roll out each piece of dough between 2 sheets of baking parchment to rectangles. Brush the top of the vanilla dough with a little egg white and place the chocolate rectangle on top. Brush this with a little beaten egg white and place the almond rectangle on top. Using a sharp knife, cut into 5-mm/¼-inch thick slices, then cut each slice in half.

5. Place on the prepared baking sheets and bake for 10–12 minutes. Leave to cool for 5–10 minutes, then carefully transfer the cookies to wire racks to cool.

Makes about 20

* 225 g/8 oz butter, softened
* 140 g/5 oz caster sugar
* 1 egg yolk, lightly beaten
* 1 tsp vanilla extract
* 300 g/10½ oz plain flour
  1 tbsp cocoa powder
  ½ tsp almond extract
  few drops of green food colouring
  1 egg white, lightly beaten
* salt

34

Biscotti

1. Put the butter, sugar and lemon rind into a bowl and mix well with a wooden spoon, then beat in the egg yolk and brandy. Sift together the flour, pistachio nuts and a pinch of salt into the mixture and stir until thoroughly combined. Shape the mixture into a log, flatten slightly, wrap in clingfilm and chill in the refrigerator for 30–60 minutes.

2. Preheat the oven to 190°C/375°F/Gas Mark 5. Line 2 baking sheets with baking parchment.

3. Unwrap the log and cut it slightly on the diagonal into 5-mm/¼-inch slices with a sharp serrated knife. Put them on the prepared baking sheets spaced well apart.

4. Bake for 10 minutes, until golden brown. Leave to cool on the baking sheets for 5–10 minutes, then using a palette knife, carefully transfer to wire racks to cool completely. Dust with icing sugar.

Makes about 30

* 225 g/8 oz butter, softened
* 140 g/5 oz caster sugar
  finely grated rind of 1 lemon
* 1 egg yolk, lightly beaten
  2 tsp brandy
* 280 g/10 oz plain flour
  85 g/3 oz pistachio nuts
* salt
  icing sugar, for dusting

Golden Hazelnut Cookies

1. Put the butter and sugar into a bowl and mix well with a wooden spoon, then beat in the egg yolk. Sift together the flour and a pinch of salt into the mixture, add the ground hazelnuts and stir until thoroughly combined. Halve the dough, form into balls, wrap in clingfilm and chill in the refrigerator for 30–60 minutes.

2. Preheat the oven to 190°C/375°F/Gas Mark 5. Line 2 baking sheets with baking parchment,

3. Unwrap the dough and roll out between 2 sheets of baking parchment. Stamp out rounds with a plain 6-cm/2½-inch cutter and put them on the prepared baking sheet spaced well apart.

4. Bake for 10–12 minutes, until golden brown. Leave to cool for 5-10 minutes, then carefully transfer the cookies to wire racks to cool.

5. When the cookies are cool, place the wire racks over a sheet of baking parchment. Put the chocolate into a heatproof bowl and melt over a pan of gently simmering water. Remove the bowl from the heat and leave to cool, then spoon the chocolate over the cookies. Gently tap the wire racks to level the surface and leave to set.

6. Add a hazelnut to the centre of each cookie and leave to set.

Makes about 30

* 225 g/8 oz butter, softened
* 140 g/5 oz golden caster sugar
* 1 egg yolk, lightly beaten
* 225 g/8 oz plain flour
  55 g/2 oz ground hazelnuts
* salt

To decorate
225 g/8 oz plain chocolate, broken into pieces
about 30 hazelnuts

Apricot & Pecan Cookies

1. Put the butter and sugar into a bowl and mix well with a wooden spoon, then beat in the egg yolk and vanilla extract. Sift together the flour and a pinch of salt into the mixture, add the orange rind and apricots and stir until thoroughly combined. Shape the dough into a log. Spread out the pecans in a shallow dish. Roll the log in the nuts until well coated, then wrap in clingfilm and chill in the refrigerator for 30–60 minutes.

2. Preheat the oven to 190°C/375°F/Gas Mark 5. Line 2 baking sheets with baking parchment.

3. Unwrap the dough and cut into 5-mm/¼-inch slices with a sharp serrated knife. Put the slices on the prepared baking sheets spaced well apart.

4. Bake for 10–12 minutes. Leave to cool on the baking sheets for 5–10 minutes, then using a palette knife, carefully transfer to wire racks to cool completely.

Makes about 30

* 225 g/8 oz butter, softened
* 140 g/5 oz caster sugar
* 1 egg yolk, lightly beaten
* 2 tsp vanilla extract
* 280 g/10 oz plain flour
  grated rind of 1 orange
  55 g/2 oz ready-to-eat dried apricots, chopped
  100 g/3½ oz pecan nuts, finely chopped
* salt

37

Pistachio & Almond Cookies

1. Put the butter and sugar into a bowl and mix well with a wooden spoon, then beat in the egg yolk and almond extract. Sift together the flour and a pinch of salt into the mixture, add the ground almonds and stir until thoroughly combined. Halve the dough, shape into balls, wrap in clingfilm and chill in the refrigerator for 30–60 minutes.

2. Preheat the oven to 190°C/375°F/Gas Mark 5. Line 2 baking sheets with baking parchment.

3. Unwrap the dough and roll out between 2 sheets of baking parchment to about 3 mm/⅛ inch thick. Sprinkle half the pistachio nuts over each piece of dough and roll lightly with the rolling pin. Stamp out cookies with a heart-shaped cutter and place on the prepared baking sheets spaced well apart.

4. Bake for 10–12 minutes. Leave to cool on the baking sheets for 5–10 minutes, then using a palette knife, carefully transfer the cookies to wire racks to cool completely.

Makes about 30

* 225 g/8 oz butter, softened
* 140 g/5 oz caster sugar
* 1 egg yolk, lightly beaten
  2 tsp almond extract
* 225 g/8 oz plain flour
  55 g/2 oz ground almonds
  55 g/2 oz pistachio nuts, finely chopped
* salt

Cappuccino Cookies

1. Empty the cappuccino sachets into a small bowl and stir in the hot, but not boiling water to make a paste.

2. Put the butter and sugar into a bowl and mix well with a wooden spoon, then beat in the egg yolk and cappuccino paste. Sift together the flour and a pinch of salt into the mixture and stir until thoroughly combined. Halve the dough, shape into balls, wrap in clingfilm and chill in the refrigerator for 30–60 minutes.

3. Preheat the oven to 190°C/375°F/Gas Mark 5. Line 2 baking sheets with baking parchment.

4. Unwrap the dough and roll out between 2 sheets of baking parchment. Stamp out cookies with a 6-cm/2½-inch round cutter and put them on the prepared baking sheets spaced well apart.

5. Bake for 10–12 minutes, until golden brown. Leave to cool for 5-10 minutes, then carefully transfer to wire racks to cool completely.

6. When the cookies are cool, place the wire racks over a sheet of baking parchment. Put the chocolate into a heatproof bowl and melt over a pan of gently simmering water. Remove the bowl from the heat and leave to cool, then spoon the chocolate over the cookies. Gently tap the wire racks to level the surface and leave to set. Dust lightly with cocoa powder.

Makes about 30

2 sachets instant cappuccino

1 tbsp hot water

* 225 g/8 oz butter, softened
* 140 g/5 oz caster sugar
* 1 egg yolk, lightly beaten
* 280 g/10 oz plain flour

175 g/6 oz white chocolate, broken into pieces

* salt

cocoa powder, for dusting

Camomile Cookies

1. Put the butter and sugar into a bowl and mix well with a wooden spoon. If necessary, remove the tea leaves from the tea bags. Stir the tea into the butter mixture, then beat in the egg yolk and vanilla extract. Sift together the flour and a pinch of salt into the mixture and stir until thoroughly combined.

2. Shape the dough into a log. Spread out 3–4 tablespoons of caster sugar in a shallow dish and roll the log in the sugar to coat. Wrap in clingfilm and chill for 30–60 minutes.

3. Preheat the oven to 190°C/375°F/Gas Mark 5. Line 2 baking sheets with baking parchment.

4. Unwrap the log and cut into 5-mm/¼-inch slices with a sharp serrated knife. Put them on the prepared baking sheets spread well apart.

5. Bake for about 10 minutes, until golden. Leave to cool on the baking sheets for 5–10 minutes, then using a palette knife, carefully transfer to wire racks to cool completely.

Makes about 30

* 225 g/8 oz butter, softened
* 140 g/5 oz golden caster sugar, plus extra for coating
* 1 tbsp (3–4 tea bags) camomile or camomile and lime flower infusion or tea
* 1 egg yolk, lightly beaten
* 1 tsp vanilla extract
* 280 g/10 oz plain flour
* salt

40

Cinnamon & Orange Crisps

1. Put the butter, 140 g/5 oz of the sugar and the orange rind into a bowl and mix well with a wooden spoon, then beat in the egg yolk and 2 tsp of the orange juice. Sift together the flour and a pinch of salt into the mixture and stir until thoroughly combined. Shape the dough into a ball, wrap in clingfilm and chill for 30–60 minutes.

2. Unwrap the dough and roll out between 2 sheets of baking parchment into a 30-cm/12-inch square. Brush with the remaining orange juice and sprinkle with the cinnamon. Lightly roll with the rolling pin. Roll up the dough like a Swiss roll. Wrap in clingfilm and chill in the refrigerator for 30 minutes.

3. Preheat the oven to 190°C/375°F/Gas Mark 5. Line 2 baking sheets with baking parchment.

4. Unwrap the dough and using a sharp knife, cut into thin slices. Put them on the prepared baking sheets spaced well apart and bake for 10–12 minutes. Leave to cool on the baking sheets for 5–10 minutes, then using a palette knife, carefully transfer to wire racks to cool completely.

Makes about 30

* 225 g/8 oz butter, softened
* 200 g/7 oz caster sugar
  grated rind of 1 orange
* 1 egg yolk, lightly beaten
  4 tsp orange juice
* 280 g/10 oz plain flour
  2 tsp ground cinnamon
* salt

Party

41

Chocolate & Ginger Checkerboard Cookies

1. Put the butter and sugar into a bowl and mix well with a wooden spoon, then beat in the egg yolk and vanilla extract. Sift together the flour and a pinch of salt into the mixture and stir until thoroughly combined.

2. Divide the dough in half. Add the ginger and orange rind to one half and mix well. Shape the dough into a log 15 cm/ 6 inch long. Flatten the sides and top to square off the log to 5-cm/2-inch high. Wrap in clingfilm and chill in the refrigerator for 30–60 minutes. Add the cocoa to the other half of the dough and mix well. Shape into a flattened log exactly the same size as the first one, wrap in clingfilm and chill in the refrigerator for 30–60 minutes.

3. Unwrap the dough and cut each flattened log lengthways into 3 slices. Cut each slice lengthways into 3 strips. Brush the strips with egg white and stack them in threes, alternating the flavours, to make the original flattened log shapes again. Wrap in clingfilm and chill in the refrigerator for 30–60 minutes.

4. Preheat the oven to 190°C/375°F/Gas Mark 5. Line 2 baking sheets with baking parchment.

5. Unwrap the logs and cut into slices with a sharp serrated knife. Put the cookies on the prepared baking sheets spaced well apart. Bake for 12–15 minutes, until firm. Leave to cool for 5–10 minutes, then carefully transfer to wire racks to cool completely.

Makes about 30

* 225 g/8 oz butter, softened
* 140 g/5 oz caster sugar
* 1 egg yolk, lightly beaten
* 2 tsp vanilla extract
* 280 g/10 oz plain flour
  1 tsp ground ginger
  1 tbsp finely grated orange rind
  1 tbsp cocoa powder, sifted
  1 egg white, lightly beaten
* salt

42

Iced Stars

1. Put the butter and sugar into a bowl and mix well with a wooden spoon, then beat in the egg yolk and vanilla extract. Sift together the flour and a pinch of salt into the mixture and stir until thoroughly combined. Halve the dough, shape into balls, wrap in clingfilm and chill in the refrigerator for 30–60 minutes.

2. Preheat the oven to 190°C/375°F/Gas Mark 5. Line 2 baking sheets with baking parchment.

3. Unwrap the dough and roll out between 2 sheets of baking parchment to about 3 mm/⅛ inch thick. Stamp out cookies with a star-shaped cutter and put them on the prepared baking sheets spaced well apart.

4. Bake for 10–15 minutes, until light golden brown. Leave to cool on the baking sheets for 5–10 minutes, then using a palette knife, carefully transfer to wire racks to cool completely.

5. To decorate, sift the icing sugar into a bowl and stir in 1–2 tablespoons warm water until the mixture has the consistency of thick cream. Divide the icing among 3–4 bowls and add a few drops of your chosen food colourings to each. Leave the cookies on the racks and spread the different coloured icings over them to the edges. Arrange silver and gold balls on top and/or sprinkle with hundred and thousands, etc. If you like, colour desiccated coconut with edible food colouring in a contrasting colour. Leave the cookies to set.

Makes about 30

* 225 g/8 oz butter, softened
* 140 g/5 oz caster sugar
* 1 egg yolk, lightly beaten
* ½ tsp vanilla extract
* 280 g/10 oz plain flour
* salt

To decorate
200 g/7 oz icing sugar
edible food colourings
silver and gold balls
hundreds and thousands
desiccated coconut
sugar sprinkles
sugar stars, hearts and flowers

Chocolate Buttons

1. Empty the chocolate drink sachets into a bowl and stir in the hot water to make a paste. Put the butter and sugar into a bowl and mix well with a wooden spoon, then beat in the egg yolk and chocolate paste. Sift together the flour and a pinch of salt into the mixture and stir until thoroughly combined. Halve the dough, shape into rounds, wrap in clingfilm and chill in the refrigerator for 30–60 minutes.

2. Preheat the oven to 190°C/375°F/Gas Mark 5. Line 2 baking sheets with baking parchment.

3. Unwrap the dough and roll out between 2 sheets of baking parchment to 3 mm/⅛ inch thick. Stamp out rounds with a plain 5-cm/2-inch cutter. Using a 3-cm/1¼-inch cap from a soft drink or mineral water bottle, make an indentation in the centre of each button. Using a wooden toothpick, make 4 holes in the centre of each button, then put them on the prepared baking sheets spaced well apart. Sprinkle with caster sugar.

4. Bake for 10–15 minutes, until firm. Leave to cool on the baking sheets for 5–10 minutes, then using a palette knife, transfer to wire racks to cool completely.

Makes about 30

- 2 sachets instant chocolate or fudge chocolate drink
- 1 tbsp hot water
- ✳ 225 g/8 oz butter, softened
- ✳ 140 g/5 oz caster sugar, plus extra for sprinkling
- ✳ 1 egg yolk, lightly beaten
- ✳ 280 g/10 oz plain flour
- ✳ salt

Name Cookies

1. Put the butter and sugar into a bowl and mix well with a wooden spoon, then beat in the egg yolk, orange juice or liqueur and grated rind. Sift together the flour and a pinch of salt into the mixture and stir until thoroughly combined. Halve the dough, shape into balls, wrap in clingfilm and chill in the refrigerator for 30–60 minutes.

2. Preheat the oven to 190°C/375°F/Gas Mark 5. Line 2 baking sheets with baking parchment.

3. Unwrap the dough and roll out to about 3 mm/⅛ inch thick. Depending on the occasion and age group, stamp out appropriate shapes with cookie cutters. Put the cookies on the prepared baking sheets spaced well apart.

4. Bake for 10–15 minutes, until light golden brown. Leave to cool for 5–10 minutes, then carefully transfer to wire racks to cool completely.

5. Leave the cookies on the racks. Put the egg white and icing sugar into a bowl and beat until smooth, adding a very little water if necessary (the icing should just hold its shape). Transfer half the icing to another bowl and colour each bowl of icing with a different colour.

6. Put both icings in piping bags with fine tips or into small plastic bags (see page 7). Decorate with sweets, green balls or crystallized flowers and leave to set.

Makes 25–30

* 225 g/8 oz butter, softened
* 140 g/5 oz caster sugar
* 1 egg yolk, lightly beaten
  2 tsp orange juice or orange liqueur
  grated rind of 1 orange
* 280 g/10 oz plain flour
* salt

To decorate
1 egg white
225 g/8 oz icing sugar
few drops each of 2 edible food colours
small sweets, green balls or crystallized flowers

45

Turkish Delight Cookies

1. Put the butter and sugar into a bowl and mix well with a wooden spoon, then beat in the egg yolk and almond extract. Sift together the flour and a pinch of salt into the mixture, add the pistachios and stir until thoroughly combined. Halve the dough, shape into balls, wrap in clingfilm and chill for 30–60 minutes.

2. Preheat the oven to 190°C/375°F/Gas Mark 5. Line 2 baking sheets with baking parchment.

3. Unwrap the dough and roll out between 2 sheets of baking parchment. Stamp out 6-cm/2½-inch squares and put them on the prepared baking sheets.

4. Bake for 12–15 minutes, until light golden brown, then remove from the oven. Cover the tops of the cookies with halved mini marshmallows. Brush with water and sprinkle with the coconut. Return to the oven for about 30 seconds, until the marshmallows have softened. Leave to cool on the baking sheets for 5–10 minutes, then using a palette knife, transfer the cookies to wire racks to cool completely.

Makes about 30

* 225 g/8 oz butter, softened
* 140 g/5 oz rose petal flavoured caster sugar
* 1 egg yolk, lightly beaten
  1 tsp almond extract
* 280 g/10 oz plain flour
  100 g/3½ oz pistachio nuts, chopped
  175 g/6 oz white mini marshmallows, halved horizontally
  25–55 g/1–2 oz desiccated coconut
* salt

Sugared Hearts

1. Put the butter and half the sugar into a bowl and mix well with a wooden spoon, then beat in the egg yolk and vanilla extract. Sift together the flour, cocoa powder and a pinch of salt into the mixture and stir until thoroughly combined. Halve the dough, shape into balls, wrap in clingfilm and chill in the refrigerator for 30–60 minutes.

2. Preheat the oven to 190°C/375°F/Gas Mark 5. Line 2 baking sheets with baking parchment.

3. Unwrap the dough and roll out between 2 sheets of baking parchment. Stamp out cookies with a heart-shaped cutter and put them on the prepared baking sheets spaced well apart.

4. Bake for 10–15 minutes, until firm. Leave to cool on the baking sheets for 5–10 minutes, then using a palette knife, carefully transfer to wire racks to cool completely.

5. Meanwhile, divide the remaining sugar among 4 small plastic bags or bowls. Add a little food colouring paste to each and rub in until well mixed. (Wear a plastic glove if mixing in bowls to prevent staining.) Put the chocolate in a heatproof bowl and melt over a pan of gently simmering water. Remove from the heat and leave to cool slightly.

6. Leave the cookies on the racks. Spread the melted chocolate over them and sprinkle with the coloured sugar. Leave to set.

Makes about 30

* 225 g/8 oz butter, softened
* 280 g/10 oz caster sugar
* 1 egg yolk, lightly beaten
* 2 tsp vanilla extract
* 250 g/9 oz plain flour
* 25 g/1 oz cocoa powder
* 3–4 food colouring pastes
* 100 g/3½ oz plain chocolate, broken into pieces
* salt

Chocolate Dominoes

1. Put the butter and sugar into a bowl and mix well with a wooden spoon, then beat in the egg yolk and vanilla extract. Sift together the flour, cocoa powder and a pinch of salt into the mixture, add the coconut and stir until thoroughly combined. Halve the dough, shape into balls, wrap in clingfilm and chill in the refrigerator for 30–60 minutes.

2. Preheat the oven to 190°C/375°F/Gas Mark 5. Line 2 baking sheets with baking parchment.

3. Unwrap the dough and roll out between 2 sheets of baking parchment. Stamp out cookies with a 9-cm/3½-inch plain square cutter, then cut them in half to make rectangles. Put them on the prepared baking sheets and using a knife, make a line across the centre of each without cutting through. Arrange the chocolate chips on top of the cookies to look like dominoes, pressing them in gently.

4. Bake for 10–15 minutes, until golden brown. Leave to cool on the baking sheets for 5–10 minutes, then using a palette knife, carefully transfer to wire racks to cool completely.

Makes 28

- 225 g/8 oz butter, softened
- 140 g/5 oz caster sugar
- 1 egg yolk, lightly beaten
- 2 tsp vanilla extract
- 250 g/9 oz plain flour
- 25 g/1 oz cocoa powder
- 25 g/1 oz desiccated coconut
- 50 g/1¾ oz white chocolate chips
- salt

48

Painted Ladies

1. Put the malted drink in a bowl and stir in the hot, but not boiling water to make a paste.

2. Put the butter and sugar into a bowl and mix well with a wooden spoon, then beat in the egg yolk and malted drink paste. Sift together the flour and a pinch of salt into the mixture and stir until thoroughly combined. Halve the dough, shape into balls, wrap in clingfilm and chill in the refrigerator for 30–60 minutes.

3. Preheat the oven to 190°C/375°F/Gas Mark 5. Line 2 baking sheets with baking parchment.

4. Unwrap the dough and roll out between 2 sheets of baking parchment. Stamp out cookies with a butterfly cutter and put them on the prepared baking sheets.

5. Whisk an egg yolk and put a little of it in an egg cup. Add a few drops of food colouring and mix well. Using a fine paintbrush, paint a pattern on the butterflies' wings. Mix other colours with beaten egg yolk in egg cups and add to the pattern.

6. Bake for 10–15 minutes, until firm. Leave to cool on the baking sheets for 5–10 minutes, then using a palette knife, carefully transfer to wire racks to cool completely.

Makes about 20

2 sachets instant malted food drink
1 tbsp hot water
225 g/8 oz butter, softened
140 g/5 oz caster sugar
1 egg yolk, lightly beaten
280 g/10 oz plain flour
salt

To decorate
egg yolks
edible food colouring

Margarita Cookies

1. Preheat the oven to 190°C/375°F/Gas Mark 5. Line 2 baking sheets with baking parchment.

2. Put the butter, sugar and lime rind into a bowl and mix well with a wooden spoon, then beat in the egg yolk and orange liqueur or orange extract. Sift together the flour and a pinch of salt into the mixture and stir until thoroughly combined.

3. Scoop up tablespoons of the dough and put them on the prepared baking sheets, then flatten gently. Bake for 10–15 minutes, until light golden brown. Leave to cool on the baking sheets for 5–10 minutes, then using a palette knife, carefully transfer to wire racks to cool completely.

4. Sift the icing sugar into a bowl and stir in sufficient tequila to give the mixture the consistency of thick cream. Leave the cookies on the racks and drizzle the icing over them with a teaspoon. Leave to set.

Makes about 30

* 225 g/8 oz butter, softened
* 140 g/5 oz caster sugar
  finely grated rind of 1 lime
* 1 egg yolk, lightly beaten
  2 tsp orange liqueur or 1 tsp orange extract
* 280 g/10 oz plain flour
* salt

To decorate
140 g/5 oz icing sugar
2 tbsp white tequila

Peach Daiquiri Cookies

1. Preheat the oven to 190°C/375°F/Gas Mark 5. Line 2 baking sheets with baking parchment.

2. Put the butter, sugar and lime rind into a bowl and mix well with a wooden spoon, then beat in the egg yolk and rum. Sift together the flour, dried peach and a pinch of salt into the mixture and stir until thoroughly combined.

3. Scoop up tablespoons of the dough and put them on the prepared baking sheets, then flatten gently. Bake for 10–15 minutes, until light golden brown. Leave to cool on the baking sheets for 5–10 minutes, then using a palette knife, carefully transfer to wire racks to cool completely.

4. Sift the icing sugar into a bowl and stir in sufficient rum to give the mixture the consistency of thick cream. Leave the cookies on the racks and drizzle the icing over them with a teaspoon. Leave to set.

Makes about 30

* 225 g/8 oz butter, softened
* 140 g/5 oz caster sugar
  finely grated rind of 1 lime
* 1 egg yolk, lightly beaten
  2 tsp white rum
* 280 g/10 oz plain flour
  100 g/3½ oz ready-to-eat dried peach, chopped
* salt

To decorate
140 g/5 oz icing sugar
2 tbsp white rum

51

Classic Saffron Cookies

1. Put the currants in a bowl, pour in the wine and leave to soak for 1 hour. Drain the currants and reserve any remaining wine.

2. Preheat the oven to 190°C/375°F/Gas Mark 5. Line 2 baking sheets with baking parchment.

3. Put the butter and sugar into a bowl and mix well with a wooden spoon, then beat in the egg yolk and 2 tsp of the reserved wine. Sift together the flour, saffron and a pinch of salt into the mixture and stir until thoroughly combined.

4. Scoop up tablespoons of the dough and put them on the prepared baking sheets spaced well apart. Flatten gently and smooth the tops with the back of the spoon.

5. Bake for 10–15 minutes, until light golden brown. Leave to cool on the baking sheets for 5–10 minutes, then using a palette knife, carefully transfer to wire racks to cool completely.

Makes about 30

100 g/3½ oz currants
125 ml/4 fl oz sweet white wine
225 g/8 oz butter, softened
140 g/5 oz caster sugar
1 egg yolk, lightly beaten
280 g/10 oz plain flour
½ tsp powdered saffron
salt

Caribbean Cookies

1. Preheat the oven to 190°C/375°F/Gas Mark 5. Line 2 baking sheets with baking parchment.

2. Put the butter and sugar into a bowl and mix well with a wooden spoon, then beat in the egg yolk and rum or rum flavouring. Sift together the flour and a pinch of salt into the mixture, add the coconut and stir until thoroughly combined.

3. Scoop up tablespoons of the dough and put them on the prepared baking sheets spaced well apart. Make a hollow in the centre of each with the dampened handle of a wooden spoon. Fill the hollows with lime marmalade.

4. Bake for 10–15 minutes, until light golden brown. Leave to cool on the baking sheets for 5–10 minutes, then using a palette knife, carefully transfer to wire racks to cool completely.

Makes about 30

- 225 g/8 oz butter, softened
- 140 g/5 oz caster sugar
- 1 egg yolk, lightly beaten
- 2 tsp rum or rum flavouring
- 280 g/10 oz plain flour
- 100 g/3½ oz desiccated coconut
- 4 tbsp lime marmalade
- salt

Patriotic Cookies

1. Preheat the oven to 190°C/375°F/Gas Mark 5. Line 2 baking sheets with baking parchment.

2. Put the butter and sugar into a bowl and mix well with a wooden spoon, then beat in the egg yolk and orange juice. Sift together the flour and a pinch of salt into the mixture, add the blueberries, cranberries and chocolate chips and stir until thoroughly combined. Scoop up tablespoons of the dough and put them on the prepared baking sheets spaced well apart.

3. Bake for 10–15 minutes, until light golden brown. Leave to cool on the baking sheets for 5–10 minutes, then using a palette knife, carefully transfer to wire racks to cool completely.

Makes about 30

- 225 g/8 oz butter, softened
- 140 g/5 oz golden caster sugar
- 1 egg yolk, lightly beaten
  2 tsp orange juice
- 280 g/10 oz plain flour
  55 g/2 oz fresh or dried blueberries
  55 g/2 oz fresh or dried cranberries
  25 g/1 oz white chocolate chips
- salt

54

Double Heart Cookies

1. Put the instant latte into a small bowl and stir in the hot, but not boiling water to make a paste.

2. Put the butter and sugar into a bowl and mix well with a wooden spoon, then beat in the egg yolk. Divide the mixture in half. Beat the latte paste into one half. Sift 140 g/5 oz of the flour with a pinch of salt into the mixture and stir until thoroughly combined. Shape the dough into a ball, wrap in clingfilm and chill in the refrigerator for 30–60 minutes.

3. Beat the vanilla extract into the other bowl, then sift together the remaining flour, the cocoa powder and a pinch of salt into the mixture. Stir until thoroughly combined. Shape the dough into a ball, wrap in clingfilm and chill in the refrigerator for 30–60 minutes.

4. Preheat the oven to 190°C/375°F/Gas Mark 5. Line 2 baking sheets with baking parchment.

5. Unwrap both flavours of dough and roll out each between 2 sheets of baking parchment. Stamp out cookies with a 7-cm/2¾-inch heart-shaped cutter and put them on the prepared baking sheets spaced well apart. Using a 4–5-cm/1½–2-inch heart-shaped cutter, stamp out the centres of each larger heart and remove from the baking sheets. Put a small chocolate-flavoured heart in the centre of each large coffee-flavoured heart and vice versa. Bake for 10–15 minutes. Leave to cool for 5–10 minutes, then carefully transfer to wire racks to cool completely.

Makes about 30

1 sachet instant latte
1½ tsp hot water
225 g/8 oz butter, softened
140 g/5 oz caster sugar
1 egg yolk, lightly beaten
250 g/9 oz plain flour
1 tsp vanilla extract
3 tbsp cocoa powder
salt

Easter Nest Cookies

1. Put the butter and sugar into a bowl and mix well with a wooden spoon, then beat in the egg yolk and lemon juice. Sift together the flour and a pinch of salt into the mixture, add the mixed peel and glacé cherries and stir until thoroughly combined. Halve the dough, shape into balls, wrap in clingfilm and chill in the refrigerator for 30–60 minutes.

2. Preheat the oven to 190°C/375°F/Gas Mark 5. Generously grease round-based bun tins with butter.

3. Unwrap the dough and roll out between 2 sheets of baking parchment. Stamp out cookies with a 7–8-cm/2¾–3¼-inch sun-shaped cutter and put them in the prepared tins.

4. Bake for 10–15 minutes, until light golden brown. Leave to cool in the tins.

5. Sift the icing sugar into a bowl, add the food colouring and stir in just enough water to give the icing the consistency of thick cream. Put the cookies on wire racks and gently spread the icing on them. When it is just beginning to set, gently press 3–4 eggs into it and sprinkle the sugar sprinkles around them. Leave to set completely.

Makes about 20–25

* 225 g/8 oz butter, softened, plus extra for greasing
* 140 g/5 oz caster sugar
* 1 egg yolk, lightly beaten
  2 tsp lemon juice
* 280 g/10 oz plain flour
  1 tbsp chopped mixed peel
  55 g/2 oz glacé cherries, finely chopped
* salt

To decorate
200 g/7 oz icing sugar
few drops of edible yellow food colouring
mini sugar-coated Easter eggs
yellow sugar sprinkles

Easter Bunny Cookies

1. Put the butter and sugar into a bowl and mix well with a wooden spoon, then beat in the egg yolk and vanilla extract. Sift together the flour, cocoa powder and a pinch of salt into the mixture, add the ginger and stir until thoroughly combined. Halve the dough, shape into balls, wrap in clingfilm and chill in the refrigerator for 30–60 minutes.

2. Preheat the oven to 190°C/375°F/Gas Mark 5. Line 2 baking sheets with baking parchment.

3. Unwrap the dough and roll out between 2 sheets of baking parchment. Stamp out 15 rounds with a 5-cm/2-inch plain cutter (bodies), 15 rounds with a 3-cm/1¼-inch plain cutter (heads), 30 rounds with a 2-cm/¾-inch plain cutter (ears) and 15 rounds with a 1-cm/½-inch plain cutter (tails). Make up the bunnies on the baking sheets spaced well apart.

4. Bake for 7 minutes, then brush the bunnies with egg white and sprinkle with caster sugar. Return to the oven and bake for a further 5–8 minutes. Remove from the oven and put a mini marshmallow in the centre of each tail. Return to the oven for 1 minute. Leave to cool for 5–10 minutes, then carefully transfer to wire racks to cool completely.

5. Sift the icing sugar into a bowl and stir in enough water to give the icing the consistency of thick cream. Add a few drops of food colouring. Pipe a collar where the heads and bodies join and add initials if desired. Leave to set.

Makes about 15

* 225 g/8 oz butter, softened
* 140 g/5 oz caster sugar, plus extra for sprinkling
* 1 egg yolk, lightly beaten
* 2 tsp vanilla extract
* 250 g/9 oz plain flour
  25 g/1 oz cocoa powder
  2 tbsp finely chopped stem ginger
  1 egg white, lightly beaten
  15 white mini marshmallows
  140 g/5 oz icing sugar
  few drops of edible pink food colouring
* salt

57

Traditional Easter Cookies

1. Put the butter and sugar into a bowl and mix well with a wooden spoon, then beat in the egg yolk. Sift together the flour, mixed spice and a pinch of salt into the mixture, add the mixed peel and currants and stir until thoroughly combined. Halve the dough, shape into balls, wrap in clingfilm and chill in the refrigerator for 30–60 minutes.

2. Preheat the oven to 190°C/375°F/Gas Mark 5. Line 2 baking sheets with baking parchment.

3. Unwrap the dough and roll out between 2 sheets of baking parchment. Stamp out cookies with a 6-cm/2½-inch fluted round cutter and put them on the prepared baking sheets spaced well apart.

4. Bake for 7 minutes, then brush with the egg white and sprinkle with caster sugar. Return to the oven and bake for a further 5–8 minutes, until light golden brown. Leave to cool on the baking sheets for 5–10 minutes, then using a palette knife, carefully transfer to wire racks to cool completely.

Makes about 30

* 225 g/8 oz butter, softened
* 140 g/5 oz caster sugar, plus extra for sprinkling
* 1 egg yolk, lightly beaten
* 280 g/10 oz plain flour
  1 tsp mixed spice
  1 tbsp mixed peel
  55 g/2 oz currants
  1 egg white, lightly beaten
* salt

Halloween Spider's Web Cookies

1. Put the butter and sugar into a bowl and mix well, then beat in the egg yolk and peppermint extract. Sift together the flour, cocoa powder and a pinch of salt into the mixture and stir until thoroughly combined. Halve the dough, shape into balls, wrap in clingfilm and chill in the refrigerator for 30–60 minutes.

2. Preheat the oven to 190°C/375°F/Gas Mark 5. Line 2 baking sheets with baking parchment.

3. Unwrap the dough and roll out between 2 sheets of baking parchment. Stamp out cookies with a 6-cm/2½-inch plain round cutter and put them on the prepared baking sheets spaced well apart.

4. Bake for 10–15 minutes, until light golden brown. Leave to cool for 5–10 minutes, then using a palette knife, carefully transfer to wire racks to cool completely.

5. Sift the icing sugar into a bowl, add the vanilla extract and stir in the hot water until the icing is smooth and has the consistency of thick cream. Leave the cookies on the racks and spread the white icing over them. Add a few drops of black food colouring to the remaining icing and spoon it into a piping bag with a fine nozzle. Starting from the middle of the cookie, pipe a series of concentric circles. Then carefully draw a cocktail stick through the icing from the middle to the outside edge to divide the cookie first into quarters and then into eighths. Leave to set.

Makes about 30

* 225 g/8 oz butter, softened
* 140 g/5 oz caster sugar
* 1 egg yolk, lightly beaten
  1 tsp peppermint extract
* 250 g/9 oz plain flour
  25 g/1 oz cocoa powder
* salt

To decorate
175 g/6 oz icing sugar
few drops of vanilla extract
1–1½ tbsp hot water
few drops of edible black food colouring

Christmas Angels

1. Put the butter and sugar into a bowl and mix well with a wooden spoon, then beat in the egg yolk and passion fruit pulp. Sift together the flour and a pinch of salt into the mixture, add the coconut and stir until thoroughly combined. Halve the dough, shape into balls, wrap in clingfilm and chill in the refrigerator for 30–60 minutes.

2. Preheat the oven to 190°C/375°F/Gas Mark 5. Line 2 baking sheets with baking parchment.

3. Unwrap the dough and roll out between 2 sheets of baking parchment. Stamp out cookies with a 7-cm/2¾-inch angel-shaped cutter and put them on the prepared baking sheets spaced well apart.

4. Bake for 10–15 minutes, until light golden brown. Leave to cool on the baking sheets for 5–10 minutes, then using a palette knife, carefully transfer to wire racks to cool completely.

5. Sift the icing sugar into a bowl and stir in the passion fruit pulp until the icing has the consistency of thick cream. Leave the cookies on the racks and spread the icing over them. Sprinkle with the edible glitter and leave to set.

Makes about 25

* 225 g/8 oz butter, softened
* 140 g/5 oz caster sugar
* 1 egg yolk, lightly beaten
  2 tsp passion fruit pulp
* 280 g/10 oz plain flour
  55 g/2 oz desiccated coconut
* salt

To decorate
175 g/6 oz icing sugar
1–1½ tbsp passion fruit pulp
edible silver glitter, for sprinkling

60

Christmas Bells

1. Put the butter, sugar and lemon rind into a bowl and mix well with a wooden spoon, then beat in the egg yolk. Sift together the flour, cinnamon and a pinch of salt into the mixture, add the chocolate chips and stir until thoroughly combined. Halve the dough, shape into balls, wrap in clingfilm and chill in the refrigerator for 30–60 minutes.

2. Preheat the oven to 190°C/375°F/Gas Mark 5. Line 2 baking sheets with baking parchment.

3. Unwrap the dough and roll out between 2 sheets of baking parchment. Stamp out cookies with a 5-cm/2-inch bell-shaped cutter and put them on the prepared baking sheets spaced well apart.

4. Bake for 10–15 minutes, until light golden brown. Leave to cool on the baking sheets for 5–10 minutes, then using a palette knife, carefully transfer to wire racks to cool completely.

5. Mix together the egg white and lemon juice in a bowl, then gradually beat in the icing sugar until smooth. Leave the cookies on the racks and spread the icing over them. Place a silver ball on the clapper shape at the bottom of the cookie and leave to set completely. When the icing is dry, use the food colouring pens to draw patterns on the cookies.

Makes about 30

* 225 g/8 oz butter, softened
* 140 g/5 oz caster sugar
  finely grated rind of 1 lemon
* 1 egg yolk, lightly beaten
* 280 g/10 oz plain flour
  ½ tsp ground cinnamon
  100 g/3½ oz plain chocolate chips
* salt

To decorate
2 tbsp lightly beaten egg white
2 tbsp lemon juice
225 g/8 oz icing sugar
30 silver balls
food colouring pens

61

Christmas Tree Decorations

1. Put the butter and sugar into a bowl and mix well with a wooden spoon, then beat in the egg yolk and vanilla extract. Sift together the flour and a pinch of salt into the mixture and stir until thoroughly combined. Halve the dough, shape into balls, wrap in clingfilm and chill in the refrigerator for 30–60 minutes.

2. Preheat the oven to 190°C/375°F/Gas Mark 5. Line 2 baking sheets with baking parchment.

3. Unwrap the dough and roll out between 2 sheets of baking parchment. Stamp out cookies with Christmas-themed cutters and put them on the prepared baking sheets spaced well apart. Using the end of a large plain piping nozzle, stamp out rounds from each shape and remove them. Make a small hole in the top of each cookie with a skewer so that they can be threaded with ribbon. Brush with egg white and sprinkle with hundreds and thousands. Bake for 7 minutes.

4. Meanwhile, lightly crush the sweets by tapping them with a rolling pin. Unwrap and sort into separate bowls by colour.

5. Remove the cookies from the oven and fill the holes with the crushed sweets. Return to the oven and bake for a further 5–8 minutes, until the cookies are light golden brown and the sweets have melted and filled the holes. Leave to cool. Thread thin ribbon through the holes in the top and hang.

Makes 20–25

* 225 g/8 oz butter, softened
* 140 g/5 oz caster sugar
* 1 egg yolk, lightly beaten
* 2 tsp vanilla extract
* 280 g/10 oz plain flour
* 1 egg white, lightly beaten
* 2 tbsp hundreds and thousands
* 400 g/14 oz fruit-flavoured boiled sweets in different colours
* salt

Fruity

62

Mixed Fruit Cookies

1. Put the butter and sugar into a bowl and mix well with a wooden spoon, then beat in the egg yolk. Sift together the flour, mixed spice and a pinch of salt into the mixture, add the apple, pear, prunes and orange rind and stir until thoroughly combined. Shape the dough into a log, wrap in clingfilm and chill in the refrigerator for 30–60 minutes.

2. Preheat the oven to 190°C/375°F/Gas Mark 5. Line 2 baking sheets with baking parchment.

3. Unwrap the log and cut it into 5-mm/¼-inch thick slices with a sharp serrated knife. Put them on the prepared baking sheets spaced well apart.

4. Bake for 10–15 minutes, until golden brown. Leave to cool on the baking sheets for 5–10 minutes, then using a palette knife, carefully transfer the cookies to wire racks to cool completely.

Makes about 30

* 225 g/8 oz butter, softened
* 140 g/5 oz caster sugar
* 1 egg yolk, lightly beaten
* 280 g/10 oz plain flour
  ½ tsp mixed spice
  25 g/1 oz ready-to-eat dried apple, chopped
  25 g/1 oz ready-to-eat dried pear, chopped
  25 g/1 oz ready-to-eat prunes, chopped
  grated rind of 1 orange
* salt

Chocolate & Apricot Cookies

1. Put the butter and sugar into a bowl and mix well with a wooden spoon, then beat in the egg yolk and amaretto liqueur. Sift together the flour and a pinch of salt into the mixture, add the chocolate chips and apricots and stir until thoroughly combined.

2. Shape the mixture into a log. Spread out the almonds in a shallow dish and roll the log in them to coat. Wrap in clingfilm and chill in the refrigerator for 30–60 minutes.

3. Preheat the oven to 190°C/375°F/Gas Mark 5. Line 2 baking sheets with baking parchment.

4. Unwrap the dough and cut into 5-mm/¼-inch slices with a sharp serrated knife. Put them on the prepared baking sheets spaced well apart.

5. Bake for 12–15 minutes, until golden brown. Leave to cool on the baking sheets for 5–10 minutes, then using a palette knife, carefully transfer to wire racks to cool completely.

Makes about 30

- 225 g/8 oz butter, softened
- 140 g/5 oz caster sugar
- 1 egg yolk, lightly beaten
- 2 tsp amaretto liqueur
- 280 g/10 oz plain flour
- 55 g/2 oz dark chocolate chips
- 55 g/2 oz ready-to-eat dried apricots, chopped
- 100 g/3½ oz blanched almonds, chopped
- salt

Pear & Pistachio Cookies

1. Preheat the oven to 190°C/375°F/Gas Mark 5. Line 2 baking sheets with baking parchment.

2. Put the butter and sugar into a bowl and mix well with a wooden spoon, then beat in the egg yolk and vanilla extract. Sift together the flour and a pinch of salt into the mixture, add the pears and pistachios and stir until thoroughly combined.

3. Scoop up tablespoons of the mixture and roll into balls. Put them on the prepared baking sheets spaced well apart and flatten slightly. Gently press a whole pistachio nut into the centre of each cookie.

4. Bake for 10–15 minutes, until golden brown. Leave to cool on the baking sheets for 5–10 minutes, then using a palette knife, carefully transfer to wire racks to cool completely.

Makes about 30

* 225 g/8 oz butter, softened
* 140 g/5 oz caster sugar
* 1 egg yolk, lightly beaten
* 2 tsp vanilla extract
* 280 g/10 oz plain flour
  55 g/2 oz ready-to-eat dried pears, finely chopped
  55 g/2 oz pistachio nuts, chopped
* salt
  whole pistachio nuts, to decorate

Orange & Lemon Cookies

1. Put the butter and sugar into a bowl and mix well with a wooden spoon, then beat in the egg yolk. Sift together the flour and a pinch of salt into the mixture and stir until thoroughly combined. Halve the dough and gently knead the orange rind into one half and the lemon rind into the other. Shape into balls, wrap in clingfilm and chill in the refrigerator for 30–60 minutes.

2. Preheat the oven to 190°C/375°F/Gas Mark 5. Line 2 baking sheets with baking parchment.

3. Unwrap the orange-flavoured dough and roll out between 2 sheets of baking parchment. Stamp out rounds with a 6-cm/2½-inch cutter and put them on a prepared baking sheet spaced well apart. Repeat with the lemon-flavoured dough and stamp out crescents. Put them on the other prepared baking sheet spaced well apart.

4. Bake for 10–15 minutes, until golden brown. Leave to cool for 5–10 minutes, then carefully transfer to wire racks to cool completely.

5. To decorate, mix together the egg white and lemon juice. Gradually beat in the icing sugar with a wooden spoon until smooth. Spoon half the icing into another bowl. Stir yellow food colouring into one bowl and orange into the other. Leave the cookies on the racks. Spread the icing over the cookies and decorate with the jelly slices. Leave to set.

Makes about 30

* 225 g/8 oz butter, softened
* 140 g/5 oz caster sugar
* 1 egg yolk, lightly beaten
* 280 g/10 oz plain flour
  finely grated rind of 1 orange
  finely grated rind of 1 lemon
* salt

To decorate
1 tbsp lightly beaten egg white
1 tbsp lemon juice
115 g/4 oz icing sugar
few drops yellow food colouring
few drops orange food colouring
about 15 lemon jelly slices
about 15 orange jelly slices

Walnut & Fig Pinwheels

1. Put the butter and 140 g/5 oz of the sugar into a bowl and mix well with a wooden spoon, then beat in the egg yolk. Sift together the flour and a pinch of salt into the mixture, add the ground walnuts and stir until thoroughly combined. Shape the dough into a ball, wrap in clingfilm and chill for 30–60 minutes.

2. Meanwhile, put the remaining sugar into a saucepan and stir in 125 ml/4 fl oz water, then add the figs, mint tea and chopped mint. Bring to the boil, stirring constantly, until the sugar has dissolved, then lower the heat and simmer gently, stirring occasionally, for 5 minutes. Remove the pan from the heat and leave to cool.

3. Unwrap the dough and roll out between 2 sheets of baking parchment into a 30-cm/12-inch square. Spread the fig filling evenly over the dough, then roll up like a Swiss roll. Wrap in clingfilm and chill in the refrigerator for 30 minutes.

4. Preheat the oven to 190°C/375°F/Gas Mark 5. Line 2 baking sheets with baking parchment.

5. Unwrap the roll and cut into thin slices with a sharp serrated knife. Put the slices on the prepared baking sheets spread well apart. Bake for 10–15 minutes, until golden brown. Leave to cool on the baking sheets for 5–10 minutes, then using a palette knife, transfer to wire racks to cool completely.

Makes about 30

- 225 g/8 oz butter, softened
- 200 g g/7 oz caster sugar
- 1 egg yolk, lightly beaten
- 225 g/8 oz plain flour
- 55 g/2 oz ground walnuts
- 280 g/10 oz dried figs, finely chopped
- 5 tbsp freshly brewed mint tea
- 2 tsp finely chopped fresh mint
- salt

Banana & Raisin Cookies

1. Put the raisins into a bowl, pour in the orange juice or rum and leave to soak for 30 minutes. Drain the raisins, reserving any remaining orange juice or rum.

2. Preheat the oven to 190°C/375°F/Gas Mark 5. Line 2 baking sheets with baking parchment.

3. Put the butter and sugar into a bowl and mix well with a wooden spoon, then beat in the egg yolk and 2 teaspoons of the reserved orange juice or rum. Sift together the flour and a pinch of salt into the mixture, add the raisins and dried bananas and stir until thoroughly combined.

4. Put tablespoons of the mixture into heaps on the prepared baking sheets spaced well apart, then flatten them gently. Bake for 12–15 minutes, until golden. Leave to cool on the baking sheets for 5–10 minutes, then using a palette knife, carefully transfer to wire racks to cool completely.

Makes about 30

25 g/1 oz raisins

125 ml/4 fl oz orange juice or rum

225 g/8 oz butter, softened

140 g/5 oz caster sugar

1 egg yolk, lightly beaten

280 g/10 oz plain flour

85 g/3 oz dried bananas, finely chopped

salt

Cherry & Chocolate Diamonds

1. Put the butter and sugar into a bowl and mix well with a wooden spoon, then beat in the egg yolk and vanilla extract. Sift together the flour and a pinch of salt into the mixture, add the glacé cherries and chocolate chips and stir until thoroughly combined. Halve the dough, shape into balls, wrap in clingfilm and chill in the refrigerator for 30–60 minutes.

2. Preheat the oven to 190°C/375°F/Gas Mark 5. Line 2 baking sheets with baking parchment.

3. Unwrap the dough and roll out between 2 sheets of baking parchment to about 3 mm/⅛ inch thick. Stamp out cookies with a diamond-shaped cutter and put them on the prepared baking sheets.

4. Bake for 10–15 minutes, until light golden brown. Leave to cool on the baking sheets for 5–10 minutes, then using a palette knife, carefully transfer to wire racks to cool completely.

Makes about 30

* 225 g/8 oz butter, softened
* 140 g/5 oz caster sugar
* 1 egg yolk, lightly beaten
* 2 tsp vanilla extract
* 280 g/10 oz plain flour
  55 g/2 oz glacé cherries, finely chopped
  55 g/2 oz milk chocolate chips
* salt

69

Grapefruit & Apple Mint Cookies

1. Put the butter and sugar into a bowl and mix well with a wooden spoon, then beat in the egg yolk and grapefruit juice. Sift together the flour and a pinch of salt into the mixture, add the grapefruit rind and chopped mint and stir until thoroughly combined. Halve the dough, shape into balls, wrap in clingfilm and chill in the refrigerator for 30–60 minutes.

2. Preheat the oven to 190°C/375°F/Gas Mark 5. Line 2 baking sheets with baking parchment.

3. Unwrap the dough and roll out between 2 sheets of baking parchment to 3 mm/⅛ inch thick. Stamp out cookies with a 5-cm/2-inch flower cutter and put them on the prepared baking sheets spaced well apart. Sprinkle with caster sugar.

4. Bake for 10-15 minutes, until golden brown. Leave to cool on the baking sheets for 5–10 minutes, then using a palette knife, carefully transfer to wire racks to cool completely.

Makes about 30

* 225 g/8 oz butter, softened
* 140 g/5 oz caster sugar, plus extra for sprinkling
* 1 egg yolk, lightly beaten
  2 tsp grapefruit juice
* 280 g/10 oz plain flour
  grated rind of 1 grapefruit
  2 tsp finely chopped fresh apple mint
* salt

Lemon & Lime Cookies

1. For the decoration, put the chocolate in a heatproof bowl and melt over a pan of gently simmering water. Remove from the heat and leave to cool slightly. Line a tray with baking parchment. Dip the strips of lime rind into the melted chocolate until well-coated, then put on the prepared tray to set.

2. Put the butter and sugar into a bowl and mix well with a wooden spoon, then beat in the egg yolk and lime juice. Sift together the flour and a pinch of salt into the mixture, add the lemon rind and stir until thoroughly combined. Halve the dough, shape into balls, wrap in clingfilm and chill in the refrigerator for 30–60 minutes.

3. Preheat the oven to 190°C/375°F/Gas Mark 5. Line 2 baking sheets with baking parchment.

4. Unwrap the dough and roll out between 2 sheets of baking parchment to 3 mm/⅛ inch thick. Stamp out rounds with a 6-cm/2½-inch plain cutter and put on the prepared baking sheets.

5. Bake for 10–15 minutes, until golden brown. Leave to cool for 5–10 minutes, then carefully transfer to wire racks to cool completely.

6. For the icing, mix together the egg white and lime juice. Gradually beat in the icing sugar until smooth. Ice the cookies and top with the chocolate-coated lime rind. Leave to set.

Makes about 30

* 225 g/8 oz butter, softened
* 140 g/5 oz caster sugar
* 1 egg yolk, lightly beaten
  2 tsp lime juice
* 280 g/10 oz plain flour
  finely grated rind of 1 lemon
* salt

To decorate
140 g/5 oz dark chocolate, broken into pieces
30 thinly pared strips of lime rind

Icing
1 tbsp lightly beaten egg white
1 tbsp lime juice
115 g/4 oz icing sugar

Mango, Coconut & Ginger Cookies

1 Put the butter and sugar into a bowl and mix well with a wooden spoon, then beat in the egg yolk and ginger syrup. Sift together the flour and a pinch of salt into the mixture, add the stem ginger and mango and stir until thoroughly combined.

2 Spread out the coconut in a shallow dish. Shape the dough into a log and roll it in the coconut to coat. Wrap in clingfilm and chill in the refrigerator for 30–60 minutes.

3 Preheat the oven to 190°C/375°F/Gas Mark 5. Line 2 baking sheets with baking parchment.

4 Unwrap the log and cut it into 5-mm/¼-inch slices with a sharp serrated knife and put them on the prepared baking sheets spaced well apart.

5 Bake for 12–15 minutes. Leave to cool on the baking sheets for 5–10 minutes, then using a palette knife, carefully transfer to wire racks to cool completely.

Makes about 30

* 225 g/8 oz butter, softened
* 140 g/5 oz caster sugar
* 1 egg yolk, lightly beaten
  55 g/2 oz stem ginger, chopped, plus 2 tsp syrup from the jar
* 280 g/10 oz plain flour
  55 g/2 oz ready-to-eat dried mango, chopped
  100 g/3½ oz desiccated coconut
* salt

72

Strawberry Pinks

1. Preheat the oven to 190°C/375°F/Gas Mark 5. Line 2 baking sheets with baking parchment.

2. Put the butter and sugar into a bowl and mix well with a wooden spoon, then beat in the egg yolk and strawberry flavouring. Sift together the flour and a pinch of salt into the mixture, add the coconut and stir until thoroughly combined.

3. Scoop up tablespoons of the mixture and roll them into balls. Put on the prepared baking sheets spaced well apart and use the handle of a wooden spoon to make a hollow in the centre of each. Fill the hollows with strawberry jam.

4. Bake for 12–15 minutes. Leave to cool on the baking sheets for 5–10 minutes, then using a palette knife, carefully transfer the cookies to wire racks to cool completely.

Makes about 30

* 225 g/8 oz butter, softened
* 140 g/5 oz caster sugar
* 1 egg yolk, lightly beaten
  1 tsp strawberry flavouring
* 280 g/10 oz plain flour
  100 g/3½ oz desiccated coconut
  4 tbsp strawberry jam
* salt

Apple Suns & Pear Stars

1. Put the butter and sugar into a bowl and mix well with a wooden spoon, then beat in the egg yolk. Sift together the flour and a pinch of salt into the mixture and stir until thoroughly combined. Transfer half the dough to another bowl.

2. Add the mixed spice and dried apple to one bowl and mix well. Shape into a ball, wrap in clingfilm and chill in the refrigerator for 30–60 minutes. Add the ginger and dried pear to the other bowl and mix well. Shape into a ball, wrap in clingfilm and chill in the refrigerator for 30–60 minutes.

3. Preheat the oven to 190°C/375°F/Gas Mark 5. Line 2 baking sheets with baking parchment.

4. Unwrap the apple-flavoured dough and roll out between 2 sheets of baking parchment to about 3 mm/⅛ inch thick. Stamp out cookies with a sun-shaped cutter and put them on a prepared baking sheet. Repeat with the pear-flavoured dough and stamp out cookies with a star-shaped cutter. Put them on the other prepared baking sheet.

5. Bake for 5 minutes, then remove the star-shaped cookies from the oven and sprinkle with the flaked almonds. Return to the oven and bake for a further 5–10 minutes. Remove the cookies from the oven but do not turn off the heat. Brush the apple suns with a little egg white and sprinkle with the demerara sugar. Return to the oven for 2–3 minutes. Leave all the cookies to cool for 5–10 minutes, then carefully transfer them to wire racks to cool completely.

Makes about 30

* 225 g/8 oz butter, softened
* 140 g/5 oz caster sugar
* 1 egg yolk, lightly beaten
* 280 g/10 oz plain flour
  ½ tsp mixed spice
  55 g/2 oz ready-to-eat dried apple, finely chopped
  ½ tsp ground ginger
  55 g/2 oz ready-to-eat dried pears, finely chopped
  25 g/1 oz flaked almonds
  1 egg white, lightly beaten
  demerara sugar, for sprinkling
* salt

Coconut & Cranberry Cookies

1. Preheat the oven to 190°C/375°F/Gas Mark 5. Line 2 baking sheets with baking parchment.

2. Put the butter and sugar into a bowl and mix well with a wooden spoon, then beat in the egg yolk and vanilla extract. Sift together the flour and a pinch of salt into the mixture, add the coconut and cranberries and stir until thoroughly combined. Scoop up tablespoons of the dough and place in mounds on the prepared baking sheets spaced well apart.

3. Bake for 12–15 minutes, until golden brown. Leave to cool on the baking sheets for 5–10 minutes, then using a palette knife, carefully transfer to wire racks to cool completely.

Makes about 30

* 225 g/8 oz butter, softened
* 140 g/5 oz caster sugar
* 1 egg yolk, lightly beaten
* 2 tsp vanilla extract
* 280 g/10 oz plain flour
  40 g/1½ oz desiccated coconut
  60 g/2¼ oz dried cranberries
* salt

75

Blueberry & Orange Cookies

1. Put the butter and sugar into a bowl and mix well with a wooden spoon, then beat in the egg yolk and orange extract. Sift together the flour and a pinch of salt into the mixture, add the blueberries and stir until thoroughly combined. Shape the dough into a log, wrap in clingfilm and chill in the refrigerator for 30–60 minutes.

2. Preheat the oven to 190°C/375°F/Gas Mark 5. Line 2 baking sheets with baking parchment.

3. Unwrap the log and cut into 5-mm/¼-inch slices with a sharp serrated knife. Put them on the prepared baking sheets spaced well apart.

4. Bake for 10–15 minutes, until golden brown. Leave to cool on the baking sheets for 5–10 minutes, then using a palette knife, carefully transfer to wire racks to cool completely.

5. Just before serving, beat the cream cheese in a bowl and stir in the orange rind. Spread the mixture over the cookies and sprinkle with the chopped nuts.

Makes about 30

* 225 g/8 oz butter, softened
* 140 g/5 oz caster sugar
* 1 egg yolk, lightly beaten
  1 tsp orange extract
* 280 g/10 oz plain flour
  100 g/3½ oz dried blueberries
  100 g/3½ oz cream cheese
  grated rind of 1 orange
  40 g/1½ oz macadamia nuts, finely chopped
* salt

Blueberry & Cranberry Cinnamon Cookies

1. Preheat the oven to 190°C/375°F/Gas Mark 5. Line 2 baking sheets with baking parchment.

2. Put the butter and sugar into a bowl and mix well with a wooden spoon, then beat in the egg yolk and vanilla extract. Sift together the flour, cinnamon and a pinch of salt into the mixture, add the blueberries and cranberries and stir until thoroughly combined.

3. Spread out the pine kernels in a shallow dish. Scoop up tablespoons of the mixture and roll them into balls. Roll the balls in the pine kernels to coat, then place on the prepared baking sheets spaced well apart and flatten slightly.

4. Bake for 10–15 minutes. Leave to cool on the baking sheets for 5–10 minutes, then using a palette knife, carefully transfer the cookies to wire racks to cool completely.

Makes about 30

* 225 g/8 oz butter, softened
* 140 g/5 oz caster sugar
* 1 egg yolk, lightly beaten
* 2 tsp vanilla extract
* 280 g/10 oz plain flour
  1 tsp ground cinnamon
  55 g/2 oz dried blueberries
  55 g/2 oz dried cranberries
  55 g/2 oz pine kernels, chopped
* salt

Date & Lemon Spirals

1. Put the butter and 140 g/5 oz of the sugar into a bowl and mix well with a wooden spoon, then beat in the egg yolk and lemon extract. Sift together the flour and a pinch of salt into the mixture and stir until thoroughly combined. Shape the dough into a ball, wrap in clingfilm and chill in the refrigerator for 30–60 minutes.

2. Meanwhile, put the dates, honey, lemon juice and lemon rind in a saucepan and stir in 125 ml/4 fl oz water. Bring to the boil, stirring constantly, then lower the heat and simmer gently, stirring occasionally, for 5 minutes. Remove from the heat and leave to cool, then chill in the refrigerator for 15 minutes.

3. Mix together the cinnamon and remaining sugar in a bowl. Unwrap the dough and roll out between 2 sheets of baking parchment into a 30-cm/12-inch square. Sprinkle the cinnamon and sugar mixture over the dough and roll lightly with the rolling pin. Spread the date mixture evenly over the dough, then roll up like a Swiss roll. Wrap in clingfilm and chill in the refrigerator for 30 minutes.

4. Preheat the oven to 190°C/375°F/Gas Mark 5. Line 2 baking sheets with baking parchment. Unwrap the roll and cut into thin slices with a sharp serrated knife. Put them on the prepared baking sheets spaced well apart. Bake for 12–15 minutes, until golden brown. Leave to cool for 5–10 minutes, then transfer to wire racks to cool completely.

Makes about 30

* 225 g/8 oz butter, softened
* 175 g/6 oz caster sugar
* 1 egg yolk, lightly beaten
* 1 tsp lemon extract
* 280 g/10 oz plain flour
* 280 g/10 oz dried dates, stoned and finely chopped
* 2 tbsp clear lemon blossom honey
* 5 tbsp lemon juice
* 1 tbsp finely grated lemon rind
* 1 tsp ground cinnamon
* salt

78

Plum & White Chocolate Cookies

1. Put the butter and sugar into a bowl and mix well with a wooden spoon, then beat in the egg yolk and vanilla extract. Sift together the flour, cocoa and a pinch of salt into the mixture and stir until thoroughly combined. Halve the dough, shape into balls, wrap in clingfilm and chill in the refrigerator for 30–60 minutes.

2. Preheat the oven to 190°C/375°F/Gas Mark 5. Line 2 baking sheets with baking parchment.

3. Unwrap a ball of dough and roll out between 2 sheets of baking parchment to about 3 mm/⅛ inch thick. Stamp out 15 rounds with a plain 5-cm/2-inch cutter and put them on the prepared baking sheets spaced well apart. Divide the chopped chocolate among the cookies. Roll out the remaining dough between 2 sheets of baking parchment and stamp out rounds with a 6–7-cm/2½–2¾-inch cutter. Place them on top of the first cookies and press the edges together to seal.

4. Bake for 10–15 minutes, until firm. Leave to cool for 5–10 minutes, then carefully transfer the cookies to wire racks to cool completely.

5. To decorate, melt the chocolate in a heatproof bowl set over a pan of gently simmering water. Remove from the heat and leave to cool slightly. Leave the cookies on the racks. Dip the cut sides of the plums into the melted chocolate and stick them in the middle of the cookies. Spoon the remaining melted chocolate over them and leave to set.

Makes about 30

* 225 g/8 oz butter, softened
* 140 g/5 oz caster sugar
* 1 egg yolk, lightly beaten
* 2 tsp vanilla extract
* 225 g/8 oz plain flour
  55 g/2 oz cocoa powder
  100 g/3½ oz white chocolate, chopped
* salt

To decorate
55 g/2 oz white chocolate, broken into pieces
15 ready-to-eat dried plums, halved

79

Papaya & Cashew Nut Cookies

1. Put the butter and sugar into a bowl and mix well with a wooden spoon, then beat in the egg yolk and lime juice. Sift together the flour and a pinch of salt into the mixture, add the papaya and stir until thoroughly combined.

2. Spread out the nuts in a shallow dish. Shape the dough into a log and roll in the cashews to coat, then wrap in clingfilm and chill in the refrigerator for 30–60 minutes.

3. Preheat the oven to 190°C/375°F/Gas Mark 5. Line 2 baking sheets with baking parchment.

4. Unwrap the dough and cut into slices with a sharp serrated knife. Put them on the prepared baking sheets spaced well apart.

5. Bake for 12–15 minutes, until light golden brown. Leave to cool on the baking sheets for 5–10 minutes, then using a palette knife, carefully transfer to wire racks to cool completely.

Makes about 30

* 225 g/8 oz butter, softened
* 140 g/5 oz caster sugar
* 1 egg yolk, lightly beaten
  2 tsp lime juice
* 280 g/10 oz plain flour
  100 g/3½ oz ready-to-eat dried papaya, chopped
  100 g/3 oz cashew nuts, finely chopped
* salt

Oaty Raisin & Hazelnut Cookies

1. Preheat the oven to 190°C/375°F/Gas Mark 5. Line 2 baking sheets with baking parchment. Put the raisins in a bowl, add the orange juice and leave to soak for 10 minutes.

2. Put the butter and sugar into a bowl and mix well with a wooden spoon, then beat in the egg yolk and vanilla extract. Sift together the flour and a pinch of salt into the mixture and add the oats and hazelnuts. Drain the raisins, add them to the mixture and stir until thoroughly combined.

3. Scoop up tablespoons of the mixture and place them in mounds on the prepared baking sheets spaced well apart. Flatten slightly and place a whole hazelnut in the centre of each cookie.

4. Bake for 12–15 minutes, until golden brown. Leave to cool on the baking sheets for 5–10 minutes, then using a palette knife, carefully transfer the cookies to wire racks to cool completely.

Makes about 30

55 g/2 oz raisins, chopped
125 ml/4 fl oz orange juice
* 225 g/8 oz butter, softened
* 140 g/5 oz caster sugar
* 1 egg yolk, lightly beaten
* 2 tsp vanilla extract
* 225 g/8 oz plain flour
55 g/2 oz rolled oats
55 g/2 oz hazelnuts, chopped
* salt
whole hazelnuts, to decorate

81

Peach, Pear & Plum Cookies

1. Preheat the oven to 190°C/375°F/Gas Mark 5. Line 2 baking sheets with baking parchment.

2. Put the butter and sugar into a bowl and mix well with a wooden spoon, then beat in the egg yolk and almond extract. Sift together the flour and a pinch of salt into the mixture, add the dried fruit and stir until thoroughly combined.

3. Scoop up tablespoons of the mixture, roll them into balls and place on the prepared baking sheets spaced well apart. Make a hollow in the centre of each with the dampened handle of a wooden spoon. Fill the hollows with the jam.

4. Bake for 12–15 minutes, until light golden brown. Leave to cool on the baking sheets for 5–10 minutes, then using a palette knife, carefully transfer to wire racks to cool completely.

Makes about 30

* 225 g/8 oz butter, softened
* 140 g/5 oz caster sugar
* 1 egg yolk, lightly beaten
  2 tsp almond extract
* 280 g/10 oz plain flour
  55 g/2 oz ready-to-eat dried peach, finely chopped
  55 g/2 oz ready-to-eat dried pear, finely chopped
  4 tbsp plum jam
* salt

Double the Fun

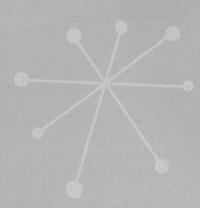

82

Jam Rings

1. Put the butter and sugar into a bowl and mix well with a wooden spoon, then beat in the egg yolk and vanilla extract. Sift together the flour and a pinch of salt into the mixture and stir until thoroughly combined. Halve the dough, shape into balls, wrap in clingfilm and chill in the refrigerator for 30–60 minutes.

2. Preheat the oven to 190°C/375°F/Gas Mark 5. Line 2 baking sheets with baking parchment.

3. Unwrap the dough and roll out between 2 sheets of baking parchment. Stamp out cookies with a 7-cm/2¾-inch fluted round cutter and put half of them on a prepared baking sheet spaced well apart. Using a 4-cm/1½-inch plain round cutter, stamp out the centres of the remaining cookies and remove. Put the cookie rings on the other baking sheet spaced well apart.

4. Bake for 7 minutes, then brush the cookie rings with beaten egg white and sprinkle with caster sugar. Bake for a further 5–8 minutes, until light golden brown. Leave to cool on the baking sheets for 5–10 minutes, then using a palette knife, carefully transfer to wire racks to cool completely.

5. To make the jam filling, beat the butter and icing sugar together in a bowl until smooth and combined. Spread the buttercream over the whole cookies and top with a little jam. Place the cookie rings on top and press gently together.

Makes about 15

* 225 g/8 oz butter, softened
* 140 g/5 oz caster sugar, plus extra for sprinkling
* 1 egg yolk, lightly beaten
* 2 tsp vanilla extract
* 280 g/10 oz plain flour
  1 egg white, lightly beaten
* salt

Jam filling
55 g/2 oz butter, softened
100 g/3½ oz icing sugar
5 tbsp strawberry or raspberry jam

Mint Cookies with White Chocolate Ganache

1. Put the butter and sugar into a bowl and mix well with a wooden spoon, then beat in the egg yolk and vanilla extract. Sift together the flour and a pinch of salt into the mixture, add the chocolate and mint sticks and stir until thoroughly combined. Halve the dough, shape into balls, wrap in clingfilm and chill in the refrigerator for 30–60 minutes.

2. Preheat the oven to 190°C/375°F/Gas Mark 5. Line 2 baking sheets with baking parchment.

3. Unwrap the dough and roll out between 2 sheets of baking parchment. Stamp out cookies with a 6-cm/2½-inch fluted round cutter and put them on the prepared baking sheets spaced well apart.

4. Bake for 10–15 minutes, until light golden brown. Leave to cool on the baking sheets for 5–10 minutes, then using a palette knife, carefully transfer to wire racks to cool completely.

5. Pour the cream into a pan, add the chocolate and melt over a low heat, stirring occasionally, until smooth. Remove the pan from the heat and leave to cool, then chill in the refrigerator until the mixture has a spreadable consistency.

6. Spread the ganache over half the cookies and top with the remaining cookies. Dust with sifted icing sugar.

Makes about 15

* 225 g/8 oz butter, softened
* 140 g/5 oz caster sugar
* 1 egg yolk, lightly beaten
* 2 tsp vanilla extract
* 280 g/10 oz plain flour
  100 g/3½ oz chocolate and mint sticks, finely chopped
* salt
  icing sugar, for dusting

White chocolate ganache
2 tbsp double cream
100 g/3½ oz white chocolate, broken into pieces

Almond Cookies with Green Tea Cream

1. Mix the butter and sugar, then beat in the egg yolk and vanilla extract. Sift in the flour and a pinch of salt and stir well. Halve the dough, wrap and chill for 30–60 minutes.

2. Preheat the oven to 190°C/375°F/Gas Mark 5. Line 2 baking sheets with baking parchment.

3. Roll out a dough ball between sheets of baking parchment. Stamp out cookies with a 6-cm/2½-inch cutter and put on a baking sheet. Roll out the other ball of dough to 1 cm/½ inch thick. Sprinkle with the almonds, re-cover with baking parchment and roll out to 5 mm/¼ inch thick. Stamp out 6-cm/2½-inch rounds and put on the other baking sheet. Brush with egg white and sprinkle with sugar. Bake for 10–15 minutes, until golden. Cool for 5–10 minutes, then transfer to wire racks.

4. For the green tea cream, bring the milk to the boil, then remove from the heat. Add the tea, cover the surface with clingfilm and infuse for 15 minutes. Strain into a clean pan. Stir in the sugar and custard powder and bring to the boil, stirring until thickened. Remove from the heat, cover the surface with clingfilm and leave to cool.

5. Beat the cream cheese until smooth. Beat in the green tea custard. Spread the cream over the plain cookies and top with the almond cookies.

Makes about 15

- ❋ 225 g/8 oz butter, softened
- ❋ 140 g/5 oz caster sugar, plus extra for sprinkling
- ❋ 1 egg yolk, lightly beaten
- ❋ 2 tsp vanilla extract
- ❋ 280 g/10 oz plain flour
- 25 g/1 oz flaked almonds
- 1 egg white, lightly beaten
- ❋ salt

Green tea cream
125 ml/4 fl oz milk

2 green tea teabags or 2 tsp green tea leaves

1 tbsp caster sugar

1 tbsp custard powder

125 g/4½ oz cream cheese

Apple & Spice Cookies

1. Put the butter and sugar into a bowl and mix well with a wooden spoon, then beat in the egg yolk and apple juice. Sift together the flour, cinnamon, mixed spice and a pinch of salt into the mixture, add the dried apple and stir until thoroughly combined. Halve the dough, shape into balls, wrap in clingfilm and chill in the refrigerator for 30–60 minutes.

2. Preheat the oven to 190°C/375°F/Gas Mark 5. Line 2 baking sheets with baking parchment.

3. Unwrap the dough and roll out between 2 sheets of baking parchment. Stamp out cookies with a 5-cm/2-inch square cutter and put them on the prepared baking sheets spaced well apart.

4. Bake for 10–15 minutes, until light golden brown. Leave to cool on the baking sheets for 5–10 minutes, then using a palette knife, carefully transfer to wire racks to cool completely.

5. To make the apple filling, mix together the caster sugar, custard powder and milk in a saucepan and bring to the boil, stirring constantly. Cook, stirring constantly, until thickened, then remove the pan from the heat and stir in the apple sauce. Cover the surface with clingfilm and leave to cool.

6. Spread the filling over half the cookies and top with the remainder.

Makes about 30

- 225 g/8 oz butter, softened
- 140 g/5 oz caster sugar
- 1 egg yolk, lightly beaten
- 2 tsp apple juice
- 280 g/10 oz plain flour
- ½ tsp ground cinnamon
- ½ tsp mixed spice
- 100 g/3½ oz ready-to-eat dried apple, finely chopped
- salt

Apple filling
- 1 tbsp caster sugar
- 1 tbsp custard powder
- 125 ml/4 fl oz milk
- 5 tbsp apple sauce

Plums & Custard Cookies

1. Put the butter and sugar into a bowl and mix well with a wooden spoon, then beat in the egg yolk and vanilla extract. Sift together the flour, custard powder and a pinch of salt into the mixture, add the plums and stir until thoroughly combined. Halve the dough, shape into balls, wrap in clingfilm and chill in the refrigerator for 30–60 minutes.

2. Preheat the oven to 190°C/375°F/Gas Mark 5. Line 2 baking sheets with baking parchment.

3. Unwrap the dough and roll out between 2 sheets of baking parchment. Stamp out cookies with a 6-cm/2½-inch fluted round cutter and put them on the prepared baking sheets spaced well apart. Using a small diamond-shaped cutter, stamp out the centres of half the cookies and remove.

4. Bake for 10–15 minutes, until light golden brown. Leave to cool on the baking sheets for 5–10 minutes, then using a palette knife, carefully transfer to wire racks to cool completely.

5. To make the custard cream, melt the butter in a small pan, then remove from the heat. Sift the icing sugar into the pan, add the milk and vanilla extract and beat well until smooth and thoroughly combined. Spread the custard cream over the whole cookies and top with the cut-out cookies.

Makes about 15

* 225 g/8 oz butter, softened
* 140 g/5 oz caster sugar
* 1 egg yolk, lightly beaten
* 2 tsp vanilla extract
* 175 g/6 oz plain flour
  115 g/4 oz custard powder
  100 g/3½ oz ready-to-eat dried plums, finely chopped
* salt

Custard cream
25 g/1 oz butter
225 g/8 oz icing sugar
2 tbsp milk
few drops of vanilla extract

Rum & Raisin Cookies with Orange Filling

1. Put the raisins in to a bowl, pour in the rum and leave to soak for 15 minutes, then drain reserving any remaining rum. Preheat the oven to 190°C/375°F/Gas Mark 5. Line 2 baking sheets with baking parchment.

2. Put the butter and sugar into a bowl and mix well with a wooden spoon, then beat in the egg yolk and 2 teaspoons of the reserved rum. Sift together the flour and a pinch of salt into the mixture, add the raisins and stir until thoroughly combined.

3. Scoop up tablespoons of the dough and put them on the prepared baking sheets spaced well apart. Flatten gently and smooth the tops with the back of a spoon.

4. Bake for 10–15 minutes, until light golden brown. Leave to cool on the baking sheets for 5–10 minutes, then using a palette knife, carefully transfer to wire racks to cool completely.

5. To make the orange filling, sift the icing sugar into a bowl, add the butter, orange rind, rum and food colouring, if using, and beat well until smooth. Spread the filling over half the cookies and top with the remaining cookies.

Makes about 30

100 g/3½ oz raisins
150 ml/5 fl oz rum
* 225 g/8 oz butter, softened
* 140 g/5 oz caster sugar
* 1 egg yolk, lightly beaten
* 280 g/10 oz plain flour
* salt

Orange filling
175 g/6 oz icing sugar
85 g/3 oz butter, softened
2 tsp finely grated orange rind
1 tsp rum
few drops of yellow edible food colouring (optional)

Redcurrant & Pastry Cream Cookies

1. Mix the butter and sugar, then beat in the egg yolk and vanilla extract. Sift in the flour and a pinch of salt and stir. Halve the dough, wrap and chill for 45 minutes.

2. Preheat the oven to 190°C/375°F/Gas Mark 5. Line 2 baking sheets with baking parchment.

3. Roll out the dough between the sheets of baking parchment. Stamp out cookies with a 6-cm/2½-inch cutter, put on the baking sheets and bake for 12 minutes, until golden. Cool for 5 minutes, then transfer to wire racks.

4. For the pastry cream, beat the egg yolk and sugar. Sift in the flours and beat well. Stir in 3 tablespoons of the milk and the vanilla extract. Bring the remaining milk to the boil, then whisk it into the mixture. Return to the pan and bring to the boil, stirring. Remove from the heat and beat until cool.

5. Stiffly whisk the egg white. Spoon a little custard into a bowl, fold in the egg white, then fold into the rest of the custard. Heat for 2 minutes, stirring, then leave to cool. Meanwhile dip the bunches of redcurrants into the egg white and roll in the caster sugar. Leave to dry.

6. Sandwich pairs of cookies together with the pastry cream. Sift the icing sugar into a bowl, stir in the lemon extract and enough warm water to make a smooth icing. Spread it on the cookies and decorate with redcurrants.

Makes about 15

- 225 g/8 oz butter, softened
- 140 g/5 oz caster sugar
- 1 egg yolk, lightly beaten
- 2 tsp vanilla extract
- 280 g/10 oz plain flour
- salt

Pastry cream
2 egg yolks, lightly beaten
4 tbsp caster sugar
1 tbsp cornflour
1 heaped tbsp plain flour
300 ml/10 fl oz milk
few drops of vanilla extract
1 egg white

To decorate
15 small bunches of redcurrants
1 egg white, lightly beaten
2–3 tbsp caster sugar
225 g/8 oz icing sugar
¼ tsp lemon extract
2 tbsp warm water

Coffee Cream & Walnut Cookies

1. Put the butter and sugar into a bowl and mix well with a wooden spoon, then beat in the egg yolk and vanilla extract. Sift together the flour and a pinch of salt into the mixture, add the ground walnuts and stir until thoroughly combined. Halve the dough, shape into balls, wrap in clingfilm and chill in the refrigerator for 30–60 minutes.

2. Preheat the oven to 190°C/375°F/Gas Mark 5. Line 2 baking sheets with baking parchment.

3. Unwrap the dough and roll out between 2 sheets of baking parchment. Stamp out cookies with a 6-cm/2½-inch fluted round cutter and put them on the prepared baking sheets spaced well apart.

4. Bake for 10–15 minutes, until light golden brown. Leave to cool on the baking sheets for 5–10 minutes, then using a palette knife, carefully transfer to wire racks to cool completely.

5. To make the coffee cream, beat the butter and icing sugar together until smooth and thoroughly combined, then beat in the coffee. Sandwich the cookies together in pairs with the coffee cream, then press together gently so that the cream oozes out of the sides. Smooth the sides with a dampened finger. Spread out the chopped walnuts in a shallow dish and roll the cookies in them to coat the sides of the coffee cream filling. Dust the tops with sifted icing sugar.

Makes about 30

- ✳ 225 g/8 oz butter, softened
- ✳ 140 g/5 oz caster sugar
- ✳ 1 egg yolk, lightly beaten
- ✳ 2 tsp vanilla extract
- ✳ 225 g/8 oz plain flour
  55 g/2 oz ground walnuts
  55 g/2 oz walnuts, finely chopped
- ✳ salt
  icing sugar, for dusting

Coffee cream
85 g/3 oz butter, softened
140 g/5 oz icing sugar
1½ tsp strong black coffee

Pineapple & Ginger Creams

1. Put the butter and sugar into a bowl and mix well with a wooden spoon, then beat in the egg yolk and vanilla extract. Sift together the flour and a pinch of salt into the mixture, add the pineapple and stir until thoroughly combined. Halve the dough, shape into balls, wrap in clingfilm and chill in the refrigerator for 30–60 minutes.

2. Preheat the oven to 190°C/375°F/Gas Mark 5. Line 2 baking sheets with baking parchment.

3. Unwrap the dough and roll out between 2 sheets of baking parchment. Stamp out cookies with a 6-cm/2½-inch fluted round cutter and put them on the prepared baking sheets spaced well apart.

4. Bake for 10–15 minutes, until light golden brown. Leave to cool on the baking sheets for 5–10 minutes, then using a palette knife, carefully transfer to wire racks to cool completely.

5. To make the ginger cream, beat the yogurt, syrup and ginger in a bowl until thoroughly combined. Sandwich the cookies together with the ginger cream. Cover half of each cookie with a piece of paper and dust the exposed half with sifted cocoa powder. Cover the cocoa-dusted half of each cookie with a piece of paper and dust the exposed half with sifted icing sugar.

Makes about 15

* 225 g/8 oz butter, softened
* 140 g/5 oz caster sugar
* 1 egg yolk, lightly beaten
* 2 tsp vanilla extract
* 280 g/10 oz plain flour
  100 g/3½ oz ready-to-eat dried pineapple, finely chopped
* salt
  cocoa powder, for dusting
  icing sugar, for dusting

Ginger cream
150 ml/5 fl oz Greek-style yogurt
1 tbsp golden syrup
1 tbsp ground ginger

91

Crunchy Nut & Honey Sandwich Cookies

1. Preheat the oven to 190°C/375°F/Gas Mark 5. Line 2 baking sheets with baking parchment.

2. Put 225 g/8 oz of the butter and the caster sugar into a bowl and mix well with a wooden spoon, then beat in the egg yolk and vanilla extract. Sift together the flour and a pinch of salt into the mixture and stir until thoroughly combined.

3. Scoop up tablespoons of the dough and roll into balls. Put half of them on a prepared baking sheet spaced well apart and flatten gently. Spread out the nuts in a shallow dish and dip one side of the remaining dough balls into them, then place on the other baking sheet, nut side uppermost, and flatten gently.

4. Bake for 10–15 minutes, until light golden brown. Leave to cool on the baking sheets for 5–10 minutes, then using a palette knife, carefully transfer to wire racks to cool completely.

5. Beat the remaining butter with the icing sugar and honey until creamy and thoroughly mixed. Spread the honey mixture over the plain cookies and top with the nut-coated cookies.

Makes about 30

* 300 g/10½ oz butter, softened
* 140 g/5 oz caster sugar
* 1 egg yolk, lightly beaten
* 2 tsp vanilla extract
* 280 g/10 oz plain flour
  40 g/1½ oz macadamia nuts, cashew nuts or pine kernels, chopped
  85 g/3 oz icing sugar
  85 g/3 oz clover or other set honey
* salt

92

Hearts & Diamonds

1. Put the butter and sugar into a bowl and mix well with a wooden spoon, then beat in the egg yolk and vanilla extract. Sift together the flour and a pinch of salt into the mixture, add the chocolate chips and stir until thoroughly combined. Halve the dough, shape into balls, wrap in clingfilm and chill in the refrigerator for 30–60 minutes.

2. Preheat the oven to 190°C/375°F/Gas Mark 5. Line 2 baking sheets with baking parchment.

3. Unwrap the dough and roll out between 2 sheets of baking parchment. Stamp out cookies with a 6-cm/2½-inch square fluted cutter and put half of them on a prepared baking sheet spaced well apart. Using small heart- and diamond-shaped cutters, stamp out the centres of the remaining cookies and remove them. Put the cookies on the other baking sheet spaced well apart.

4. Bake for 10–15 minutes. Leave to cool for 5–10 minutes, then carefully transfer to wire racks to cool completely.

5. To make the jam filling, put the jelly and lemon juice in a small saucepan and heat gently until the mixture is runny, then boil for 3 minutes. Remove the pan from the heat and leave to cool. Put the curd cheese, cream, sifted icing sugar and vanilla extract in a bowl and beat well until thoroughly combined. Spread the cream mixture over the whole cookies, add a little jelly and top with the cut-out cookies.

Makes about 30

* 225 g/8 oz butter, softened
* 140 g/5 oz caster sugar
* 1 egg yolk, lightly beaten
* 2 tsp vanilla extract
* 280 g/10 oz plain flour
  100 g/3½ oz white chocolate chips
* salt

Jam filling
5–6 tbsp redcurrant or cranberry jelly
½ tsp lemon juice
85 g/3 oz curd cheese
2 tbsp double cream
2 tsp icing sugar
few drops of vanilla extract

Clubs & Spades

1. Put the butter and sugar into a bowl and mix well with a wooden spoon, then beat in the egg yolk and vanilla extract. Sift together the flour and a pinch of salt into the mixture, add the chocolate chips and stir until thoroughly combined. Halve the dough, shape into balls, wrap in clingfilm and chill in the refrigerator for 30–60 minutes.

2. Preheat the oven to 190°C/375°F/Gas Mark 5. Line 2 baking sheets with baking parchment.

3. Unwrap the dough and roll out between 2 sheets of baking parchment. Stamp out cookies with a 6-cm/2½-inch square fluted cutter and put half of them on a prepared baking sheet spaced well apart. Using small club- and spade-shaped cutters, stamp out the centres of the remaining cookies and remove them. Put the cookies on the other baking sheet spaced well apart.

4. Bake for 10–15 minutes, until light golden brown. Leave to cool on the baking sheets for 5–10 minutes, then using a palette knife, carefully transfer to wire racks to cool completely.

5. To make the filling, put the butter and syrup into a bowl and sift in the icing sugar and cocoa powder. Beat well until smooth. Spread the chocolate cream over the whole cookies and top with the cut-out cookies.

Makes about 15

* 225 g/8 oz butter, softened
* 140 g/5 oz caster sugar
* 1 egg yolk, lightly beaten
* 2 tsp vanilla extract
* 280 g/10 oz plain flour
  100 g/3½ oz plain chocolate chips
* salt

Filling
55 g/2 oz butter, softened
1 tsp golden syrup
85 g/3 oz icing sugar
1 tbsp cocoa powder

Chocolate & Orange Cookie Sandwiches

1. Preheat the oven to 190°C/375°F/Gas Mark 5. Line 2 baking sheets with baking parchment.

2. Put the butter, sugar and orange rind into a bowl and mix well with a wooden spoon, then beat in the egg yolk and vanilla extract. Sift together the flour, cocoa powder and a pinch of salt into the mixture, add the chopped chocolate and stir until thoroughly combined.

3. Scoop up tablespoons of the dough, roll into balls and place on the prepared baking sheets spaced well apart. Gently flatten and smooth the tops with the back of a spoon.

4. Bake for 10–15 minutes, until light golden brown. Leave to cool on the baking sheets for 5–10 minutes, then using a palette knife, carefully transfer to wire racks to cool completely.

5. To make the filling, bring the cream to the boil in a small saucepan, then remove the pan from the heat. Stir in the chocolate until the mixture is smooth, then stir in the orange extract. When the mixture is completely cool, use to sandwich the cookies together in pairs.

Makes about 15

* 225 g/8 oz butter, softened
* 140 g/5 oz caster sugar
  2 tsp finely grated orange rind
* 1 egg yolk, lightly beaten
* 2 tsp vanilla extract
* 250 g/9 oz plain flour
  25 g/1 oz cocoa powder
  100 g/3½ oz plain chocolate, finely chopped
* salt

Chocolate filling
125 ml/4 fl oz double cream
200 g/7 oz white chocolate, broken into pieces
1 tsp orange extract

95

Marshmallow S'mores

1. Put the butter, sugar and orange rind into a bowl and mix well with a wooden spoon, then beat in the egg yolk. Sift together the flour, cocoa powder, cinnamon and a pinch of salt into the mixture and stir until thoroughly combined. Halve the dough, shape into balls, wrap in clingfilm and chill in the refrigerator for 30–60 minutes.

2. Preheat the oven to 190°C/375°F/Gas Mark 5. Line 2 baking sheets with baking parchment.

3. Unwrap the dough and roll out between 2 sheets of baking parchment. Stamp out cookies with a 6-cm/2½-inch fluted round cutter and put them on the prepared baking sheets spaced well apart.

4. Bake for 10-15 minutes. Leave to cool for 5 minutes. Turn half the cookies upside down and put 4 marshmallow halves on each. Return to the oven and cook for 1–2 minutes. Transfer the cookies to wire racks and leave to stand for 30 minutes.

5. Melt the chocolate in a heatproof bowl set over a pan of gently simmering water. Remove from the heat and leave to cool. Line a tray or baking sheet with baking parchment. Spread the marmalade over the undersides of the uncovered cookies and place them on top of the marshmallow-covered cookies. Dip the cookies in the melted chocolate to coat, letting the excess drip back into the bowl, then place them on the tray or baking sheet. Put a walnut half in the centre of each cookie. Leave to set.

Makes about 15

* 225 g/8 oz butter, softened
* 140 g/5 oz caster sugar
   2 tsp finely grated orange rind
* 1 egg yolk, lightly beaten
* 250 g/9 oz plain flour
   25 g/1 oz cocoa powder
   ½ tsp ground cinnamon
   30 yellow marshmallows, halved horizontally
   300 g/10½ oz dark chocolate, broken into pieces
   4 tbsp orange marmalade
   15 walnut halves
* salt

96

Tropical Fruit & Mascarpone Cream Cookie Sandwiches

1. Put the butter and sugar into a bowl and mix well with a wooden spoon, then beat in the egg yolk and passion fruit pulp. Sift together the flour and a pinch of salt into the mixture, add the mango, papaya and dates and stir until thoroughly combined. Shape the dough into a log, wrap in clingfilm and chill in the refrigerator for 30–60 minutes.

2. Meanwhile, make the mascarpone cream. Put all the ingredients in a bowl and beat with a wooden spoon until thoroughly combined and smooth. Cover the bowl with clingfilm and chill in the refrigerator.

3. Preheat the oven to 190°C/375°F/Gas Mark 5. Line 2 baking sheets with baking parchment.

4. Unwrap the dough and cut into slices with a sharp serrated knife. Put them on the prepared baking sheets spaced well apart.

5. Bake for 10–15 minutes, until light golden brown. Leave to cool on the baking sheets for 5–10 minutes, then using a palette knife, carefully transfer to wire racks to cool completely. When the cookies are cold spread the chilled mascarpone cream over half of them, sprinkle with the toasted coconut and top with the remaining cookies.

Makes about 15

* 225 g/8 oz butter, softened
* 140 g/5 oz caster sugar
* 1 egg yolk, lightly beaten
  2 tsp passion fruit pulp
* 280 g/10 oz plain flour
  40 g/1½ oz ready-to-eat dried mango, chopped
  40 g/1½ oz ready-to-eat dried papaya, chopped
  25 g/1 oz dried dates, stoned and chopped
  3–4 tbsp shredded coconut, toasted
* salt

Mascarpone cream
85 g/3 oz mascarpone cheese
3 tbsp Greek-style yogurt
7 tbsp ready-made custard
½ tsp ground ginger

97

Banana & Caramel Cookies

1. Put the butter and sugar into a bowl and mix well with a wooden spoon, then beat in the egg yolk, ginger and ginger syrup. Sift together the flour and a pinch of salt into the mixture, add the bananas and stir until thoroughly combined. Halve the dough, shape into balls, wrap in clingfilm and chill in the refrigerator for 30–60 minutes.

2. Preheat the oven to 190°C/375°F/Gas Mark 5. Line 2 baking sheets with baking parchment.

3. Unwrap the dough and roll out between 2 sheets of baking parchment. Stamp out cookies with a 6-cm/2½-inch fluted round cutter and put half of them on the prepared baking sheets spaced well apart. Place a chocolate caramel in the centre of each cookie, then top with the remaining cookies and pinch the edges of the rounds together.

4. Bake for 10–15 minutes, until light golden brown. Leave to cool on the baking sheets for 5–10 minutes, then using a palette knife, carefully transfer to wire racks to cool completely.

Makes about 30

✳ 225 g/8 oz butter, softened

✳ 140 g/5 oz caster sugar

✳ 1 egg yolk, lightly beaten

25 g/1 oz stem ginger, finely chopped, plus 2 tsp syrup from the jar

✳ 280 g/10 oz plain flour

85 g/3 oz dried bananas, finely chopped

15 chocolate caramel sweets

✳ salt

Rich Peanut, Pineapple & Cream Cheese Cookie Sandwiches

1. Set aside half the peanuts and finely chop the remainder. Put the butter and sugar into a bowl and mix well with a wooden spoon, then beat in the egg yolk. Sift together the flour, allspice and a pinch of salt into the mixture and stir until thoroughly combined. Halve the dough, shape into balls, wrap in clingfilm and chill in the refrigerator for 30–60 minutes.

2. Preheat the oven to 190°C/375°F/Gas Mark 5. Line 2 baking sheets with baking parchment.

3. Unwrap the dough and roll out between 2 sheets of baking parchment. Sprinkle evenly with the reserved peanuts and lightly roll with the rolling pin. Stamp out cookies with a 5–6-cm/2–2½-inch fluted round cutter and put them on the prepared baking sheets spaced well apart.

4. Bake for 10–15 minutes, until light golden brown. Leave to cool on the baking sheets for 5–10 minutes, then using a palette knife, carefully transfer to wire racks to cool completely.

5. Beat together the cream and cream cheese until thick and smooth. Fold in the crystallized pineapple. Spread the mixture over the undersides of half the cookies and top with the remaining cookies, peanut side uppermost.

Makes about 15

6 tbsp salted peanuts
* 225 g/8 oz butter, softened
* 140 g/5 oz caster sugar
* 1 egg yolk, lightly beaten
* 280 g/10 oz plain flour
  ½ tsp ground allspice
  3 tbsp double cream
  85 g/3 oz cream cheese
  115 g/4 oz crystallized pineapple, chopped
* salt

Chocolate Mint Cookie Sandwiches

1. Put the butter and sugar into a bowl and mix well with a wooden spoon, then beat in the egg yolk and vanilla extract. Sift together the flour, cocoa powder and a pinch of salt into the mixture, add the cherries and stir until thoroughly combined. Halve the dough, shape into balls, wrap in clingfilm and chill in the refrigerator for 30–60 minutes.

2. Preheat the oven to 190°C/375°F/Gas Mark 5. Line 2 baking sheets with baking parchment.

3. Unwrap the dough and roll out between 2 sheets of baking parchment. Stamp out cookies with a 6-cm/2½-inch plain square cutter and put them on the prepared baking sheets spaced well apart.

4. Bake for 10–15 minutes, until firm. Immediately place an after-dinner mint on top of half the cookies, then cover with the remaining cookies. Press down gently and leave to cool on the baking sheets.

5. Melt the plain chocolate in a heatproof bowl set over a pan of gently simmering water. Remove from the heat and leave to cool. Put the cookies on a wire rack over a sheet of baking parchment. Spoon the plain chocolate over them, then tap the rack to level the surface and leave to set. Melt the white chocolate in a heatproof bowl set over a pan of barely simmering water. Remove from the heat and leave to cool. Pipe or drizzle it over the cookies, then leave to set.

Makes about 15

- 225 g/8 oz butter, softened
- 140 g/5 oz caster sugar
- 1 egg yolk, lightly beaten
- 2 tsp vanilla extract
- 250 g/9 oz plain flour
- 25 g/1 oz cocoa powder
- 55 g/5 oz glacé cherries, finely chopped
- 15 after-dinner mints
- salt

Chocolate topping
- 115 g/4 oz plain chocolate, broken into pieces
- 55 g/2 oz white chocolate, broken into pieces

Ice Cream Cookie Sandwiches

1. Put the butter and sugar into a bowl and mix well with a wooden spoon, then beat in the egg yolk, ginger and ginger syrup. Sift together the flour, cocoa powder, cinnamon and a pinch of salt into the mixture and stir until thoroughly combined. Halve the dough, shape into balls, wrap in clingfilm and chill in the refrigerator for 30–60 minutes.

2. Preheat the oven to 190°C/375°F/Gas Mark 5. Line 2 baking sheets with baking parchment.

3. Unwrap the dough and roll out between 2 sheets of baking parchment. Stamp out cookies with a 6-cm/2½-inch fluted round cutter and put them on the prepared baking sheets spaced well apart.

4. Bake for 10–15 minutes, until light golden brown. Leave to cool on the baking sheets for 5–10 minutes, then using a palette knife, carefully transfer to wire racks to cool completely.

5. Remove the ice cream from the freezer about 15 minutes before serving to allow it to soften. Put a generous scoop of ice cream on half the cookies and top with the remaining cookies. Press together gently so that the filling spreads to the edges. If not serving immediately, wrap the cookies individually in foil and store in the freezer.

Makes about 30

- ✳ 225 g/8 oz butter, softened
- ✳ 140 g/5 oz golden caster sugar
- ✳ 1 egg yolk, lightly beaten
- 2 tbsp finely chopped stem ginger, plus 2 tsp syrup from the jar
- ✳ 250 g/9 oz plain flour
- 25 g/1 oz cocoa powder
- ½ tsp ground cinnamon
- 450 ml/15 fl oz vanilla, chocolate or coffee ice cream
- ✳ salt